Doug Brendel
"The Outsidah"

Ipswich UnZipped

#3 IN THE "ONLY IN IPSWICH" SERIES

TO ROSE JILLIAN!
BEST IPSWISHES!

Doug Brendel

Cover cartoon: Kristofer Brendel
Cartoon watercolors: Lydia Charlotte Brendel
Cover design and Photoshopping: Kristina Brendel
(It's a family affair.)
Inspiration: The People of Ipswich, Massachusetts

IPSWICH UNZIPPED
© 2013 by Doug Brendel
All Rights Reserved

ISBN 978-1-304-40312-4

www.DougBrendel.com

Printed in the United States of America

Dedicated to my friend,
the unofficial poet-laureate of Ipswich,
David Wallace

You must love David Wallace
A little bit of all us
Though earthbound, somehow heaven-sent
The common man, yet eloquent
That's our boy, David Wallace

You must love David Wallace
His wry reflections call us
To be as good as once we were
He's Ipswich hist'ry's connoisseur
The august David Wallace

You must love David Wallace
No, no, he isn't flawless
But such a heart is rare indeed
Let future generations heed
The words of David Wallace

You must love David Wallace
And let the world take solace
That, even though he makes his rhymes
With choices inexact and doesn't quite make the rhythm
work sometimes
There's love in David Wallace

You must love David Wallace
For when the sky is starless
When Ipswich groans for sweet relief
From taxes, snow, corruption, grief
We still have David Wallace

CONTENTS

I searched the world over, and I
decided on Ipswich.

Cool little town.

Small-town America.

Of course, there have been adjustments.

It ain't south Georgia, where I was born. Ipswich is more, uh, Yankeeish.

And it ain't Chicago, where I grew up. Chicago is big and broad-shouldered, at least according to Carl Sandburg, burly and brawling and bustling and other adjectives that start with B. Ipswich would be more of a Q-adjective town: quaint and quiet, yet quirky. And

9

quotable — especially in a really snarky debate at Town Meeting. All of which is, of course, quintessentially New Englandish.

Most of all, it ain't Phoenix, Arizona, in the heart of the Great Sonoran Desert. I spent a couple decades in that mammoth oven: one decade to thaw out from 30 Midwestern winters, and another decade turning leathery and cursing the invention of air conditioning. You realize, of course, that it was the invention of air conditioning that fooled people into thinking they could live in a desert.

Ipswich, Massachusetts, is not a desert. It has water. It has moss. Things rot here, instead of going straight to "fossil." I am spending my first New England decade re-humidifying my skin.

Of course, I will never be an "insidah." Arizona is the Land of People From Other Places. New England isn't like that. New England is the Land of People Who Have Been Here Forever. And Ipswich is the Town of People Who Have Been Here the Foreverest.

But I am happy as an "outsidah." I write a column most weeks for the local paper, commenting on life in Ipswich from the standpoint of a newcomer. This is job security: I will always be a newcomer! Each week, I try to unzip another little pocket of this wonderful place.

What you'll experience in these pages is, more or less, a year in the life of a fine New England town. Not the way it really is. Just the way it seems to me: the Outsidah.

Welcome to my town. I'm glad you're here.

Doug Brendel
Linebrook Road

ALL I WANT FOR IPSWICH

I'm not too proud to ask for what I

want. I went to the mall, I stood in line, and I climbed up on Santa's lap.

He grunted a little bit. I've got a few pounds on those three-year-olds he's used to dealing with. He shifted around under me, trying to get comfortable, or possibly it was more serious than that, and he was trying to save his spleen.

"And what would you like for Christmas, little boy?" he wheezed. I believe I detected a note of sarcasm in the "little boy" part. But I decided to ignore this. With a wish list like mine, I didn't want to risk antagonizing the jolly old elf whom I was hoping would be my provider.

I pulled a sheaf of papers out of my jacket pocket, and

unfolded them. Santa gulped.

"#1. Peace on earth."

"Ho ho ho," St. Nick answered. "You've been reading too many Hallmark cards. Let's aim a little lower, shall we?"

I sighed, but I was undeterred.

"#2. Peace in Ipswich."

Now it was Santa's turn to sigh.

"That's a lot of ground to cover, young man," he offered. "Ipswich is 42.5 square miles."

"Yeah, but 10.4 of those are water," I replied. "And more than half of Ipswich is open space. You don't have to bring peace to the open space. It's already peaceful."

"Still," Santa said, squirming, "you've got more than 13,000 people in that town. And more than 10,000 of them are registered voters. You know what that means, don't you? Ten thousand opinions. I'm not sure peace is possible. What if I just get you a puppy?"

"Never mind," I answered. "How about peace at Town Hall?"

Santa rolled his eyes. "I already brought you Robin Crosbie, and months ahead of Christmas! Aren't things more peaceful around Town Hall these days?"

"I was thinking specifically of the Board of Selectmen's room."

"Ho!" Santa bellowed. "How long have you lived here? You don't seem to understand history. As long as there are citizens' queries, there will be no peace. And if you cancel citizens' queries, you demolish 375 years of New England tradition — people would scream bloody murder. See where this leaves you? You can have peace, but they'd kill you over it."

"OK, OK," I replied. "Then maybe just peace on

Market Street."

Suddenly the twinkle returned to Kris Kringle's eyes. His cherry-red cheeks seemed to flare with a wonderful secret.

"That café owner is still yelling at his staff and throwing customers out of his restaurant?" he asked impishly.

"It's all over yelp.com," I had to admit.

"I put that guy on my naughty list every year," Santa chuckled, "but it never seems to make any difference."

He smiled broadly, almost looking through me.

"I've got good news for you, little boy," he chortled. "There's a new rum bar going in there. The keys change hands on New Year's Day."

"Wow, Santa!" I exclaimed. "Thank you!"

"Merry Christmas," he sighed happily.

Then he squeezed his eyes shut. It looked like he was about to cry.

"Santa, what's wrong!?" I cried.

"My leg is asleep," he whimpered. "Could you please get down?"

THICK, AS THIEVES

An Open Letter to the Masked Man
in Black Who Tried to Rob an Ipswich Gas Station

Friend, I want to help you. Clearly, you have issues.
According to a story in the *Boston Globe* on
November 11, you went to Haverhill first, where you
tried to rob the Peking Garden Chinese Restaurant. This
was perhaps your first mistake, because not that many
people in Haverhill love Chinese food, so there's not
going to be all that much money in the cash register.

Haverhill is more of a beer-and-pizza town. As an alternative, try Roma's, right there on Middlesex St., just off of Main; they have both an Italian and a Greek menu.

You left Peking Garden around 6 p.m., according to *Globe* Correspondent Jaclyn Reiss, but didn't show up at the Prime Energy gas station at Lord's Square in Ipswich until 9 p.m. My friend, I have not lived in Ipswich very long, but even *I* know it does not take three hours to get from Haverhill to Ipswich. What route did you take? If you stay on 97 till you get to Georgetown, then keep going straight, which actually puts you on 133 without your realizing it, you should be able to get from Peking Garden to the Prime station in about half an hour, 35 minutes tops. I imagine you got goofed up in Georgetown, didn't you? If you don't get off 97 there, you can find yourself in Beverly before you know it, crossing the bridge into Salem and wondering how the heck you got there. I sympathize, my friend. I have done this more than once.

Or perhaps you got to Ipswich in good time, but then made the mistake of stopping as you approached Lord's Square. A lot of people do this, mostly folks from Rowley. If you're going to rob the Prime station, you need to understand: the Lord's Square stop sign is not for you. This stop sign is only for people who want to proceed on High Street, perhaps to rob a funeral home or a B&B. I feel badly for you, sitting at that stop sign, with the gas station fully visible, in fact just a stone's throw away — your target in range — and yet, you can't get there. And if you drove straight past the stop sign, then realized your error, you had the additional problem of being unable to turn right on Short Street, because it's one-way going the wrong way! You must have been very,

very frustrated.

I suggest if you want to do robberies in Ipswich, get GPS. Be careful, though; your equipment may need some prep time. It took until last week for my own GPS unit to figure out which way Short Street goes.

Finally, a word about technique. Ipswich Police Sergeant Jonathan Hubbard reportedly told the *Globe* that you "showed a firearm to the gas station, but then took off." Unless this is a typo, you seem to lack a certain basic understanding of the fundamentals of gas station robbery. You cannot simply show your firearm to the gas station. You are supposed to show your firearm to the person who works at the gas station. The gas station is inanimate. It does not see your gun, it does not feel fear, and it cannot give you any money. The only thing it can do on its own is give you gasoline. Even then, you need a credit card to work the pump. And if you had a valid credit card, I guess you wouldn't be robbing gas stations.

It might be better for you to pursue another line of work. For example, we happen to have a couple openings at the moment in our school system. I can imagine a masked man in a black hood bringing a whole new dynamic to School Committee meetings. What did you get your degree in, may I ask?

FEAR AND CRAVING IN COLUMNLAND

I don't know what you expect, but

you're wrong.

You probably imagine the life of a newspaper columnist as breathtakingly glamorous, sexy even. You envision the columnist lounging about in his silk pajamas, stretched out on his velvet couch, sipping sherry, occasionally reaching over to his mahogany desk, picking up his elegant fountain pen, and scratching a few brilliantly witty and creative words as they occur to him, before returning to his repose.

I assure you, it is nothing like that. Well, hardly anything like that. I don't prefer sherry.

But it's a hard life, no matter what you think. A newspaper columnist is under constant pressure. On the one hand, there are some people ceaselessly angling to get into a column, to promote their Save-the-Knotweed campaign or spotlight Uncle Boris's dental-floss collection.

Others are simply desperate to see their name appear in print. My mailman scowls at me every Thursday as he delivers the *Chronicle*. He has already read the paper by this time, so he has been living with the terrible truth all day long: Once again this week, I have not written about my mailman. It seems to me that my mail is arriving later and later every week, and I sometimes suspect that he deliberately crumples my junk mail, as a signal of his displeasure.

On the other hand, there are people in town who recoil in horror at the very idea of their name appearing in this column. My neighbor with the yippy Pomeranian cannot get through a conversation with me without saying, "Don't write about Fluffy." He is Italian – the neighbor, not the dog – and without meaning to engage in any ugly stereotypes, I must confess that I can imagine him grunting, "Brendel sleeps with the fishes." As a matter of sheer self-preservation, I have committed never, ever to write about my neighbor's Pomeranian.

A columnist walks a tightrope every day of his life. It's a cutthroat existence. On Election Day, I was at the Y, preparing to vote. I got my ballot, looked for the first open voting booth, and headed toward it. Suddenly I heard a gruff voice behind me.

"Hey, buddy! There's a line!"

I turned around to discover that indeed, several people had arrived ahead of me and were also waiting for voting booths. They were not actually standing in a "line," they seemed to be more of a constellation, or perhaps a map of Saugus. In any case, I had mistaken them for "milling around."

"I'm so sorry," I said to the man I had offended.

But it was the woman standing next to him who spoke next. Her eyes were wide as she placed her hand on the man's elbow in a gesture of trepidation.

"This is gonna be in the newspaper next week!" she moaned to him.

The man's face went slack. I had become his worst nightmare. A columnist wields such terrible power, he can never relax. At any moment, at every turn, he has the horrible potential to alter someone's life, reshaping their destiny, and ruining their Thursday.

Good people of Ipswich, I mean you no harm. I only hope to amuse you. Please don't break my knees. I need them, praying for that dog to die.

Hurricane Sandy turned out to be terrible for East Coast residents south of us. The following column, which would have been insensitive after the fact, was written before the storm struck.

If you're reading this on Thursday,

Hurricane Sandy apparently did not pick up the offices of the *Ipswich Chronicle* and hurl them into the Atlantic Ocean.

(If you're an archeologist reading this decades later, let me explain: We had a hurricane, its name was Sandy, and it was way worse than I expected.)

As a longtime desert-dweller, I was not much concerned about Sandy's high winds. Desert rats know all about wind. We have "haboobs" — sandstorms so ferocious, they make YouTube. (Search for "Phoenix Dust Storm" and you can watch this year's massive July 21 haboob, but without having to pick the grit out of your teeth afterward.)

Wind, however, is only part of the hurricane formula. There's also this thing called "rain." Decades in the desert leave you unfamiliar with this strange phenomenon: water tumbling out of the sky. In fact, when I moved here, I had to learn not only about rain, but also about these strange contraptions known as umbrellas. Or does one say *umbrellae*? A longtime desert-dweller doesn't have a ready command of all the rain-related technical terms.

To me, this so-called umbrella appears to be a dangerous device. It's quite long and somewhat pointed, and it's way bigger than your head. Yet people actually keep them in their houses. As I understand it, this "umbrella" is designed to come between you and the falling sky-water.

Back in Phoenix, with less than nine inches of rain a year, business came to a standstill at the first sign of a raindrop. People literally stood in the doorways of storefronts to watch the rain. Children danced in the streets — my son took his skateboard out for a soggy, jolly ride — out of sheer joy, simply because this remarkable chemical compound, two parts hydrogen and one part oxygen, was falling from the heavens.

Here in Ipswich, on the other hand — as we saw this week — precip happens.

And you need an umbrella.

After the ecstasy of buying a house in Ipswich, my first shopping expedition was an umbrella hunt. To survive in the extreme environment known as New England, I understood, I would need this extreme device. I had a vague recollection of using one of these instruments long ago, perhaps in my childhood, perhaps during the Eisenhower Administration.

Soon, however, I was mortified to discover that I didn't really remember how to use an umbrella. There is no Umbrella School. If there were, they would teach you that some swoosh *out*, and others swoosh *in*. There's a spring inside the shaft of that umbrella, and the spring only *sproings* one way or the other. The key is to know, in advance, when your particular umbrella is going to strike.

And I never can remember.

Let's say I grab an umbrella from the mudroom and head to the bus stop to retrieve my fifth-grader. I certainly want to look cool for the bus stop moms. But let's say while we're waiting for the bus, it starts to rain. I grasp the umbrella handle, press the little button, and *thwack!* The umbrella jumps open, knocking me back on my heels. If any bus stop moms thought I was cool, it's all over now.

Or let's say I'm heading to a meeting, I'm a bit dressed up, I'm trying to look nice and professional for my client. It's pouring, but my trusty umbrella is keeping me dry. I arrive, I greet the pretty receptionist, I grasp the umbrella handle, I press the little button, and *shplack!* The umbrella snaps like an alligator, dousing my suit with rainwater, and splattering that expensive lamp table.

I told you (and archeologists, please note, I warned them): These things are dangerous. Possibly more dangerous than Sandy.

ROTTEN TO THE CORE

I am an unabashed Robin Crosbie

fan, but one item in the Town Manager's proposed $12.9 million five-year capital plan is simply a shock to me.

Replacement of Town Hall columns due to severe rot and insect infestation will cost $27,500.

Yes, my fellow columnists and I have written a number of Town Hall columns. But to characterize any (or all) of these columns as "severe rot" is harsher criticism than we deserve. I would say some of my own Town Hall columns have qualified as "rot," but not "severe" rot. I can remember one in particular that might have been fairly described as "near-rotten," but nothing close to "severe."

Furthermore, while I have written about insects — maybe a lot (OK, maybe too much) — I wouldn't call my columns "insect-infested." I might call them "insect-influenced." This would be fair. As far as I'm concerned, we need more attention, not less, given to the insect problems that plague Ipswich: Swarms of winter moths rising from the dead, again and again, every time New England turns the teeniest bit mild. Hoards of ladybugs marching up the sides of my house, invading my kitchen, circling my light bulbs and soup bowls like Soviet soldiers on patrol. Greenheads like stern nannies dictating our beach times. Mosquitoes turning Essex County into one huge blood donation table. Indeed, insects deserve to be called out in newspaper columns, and I for one intend to continue.

And to be precise, I have not written any insect-oriented Town Hall columns — although this is a darn good idea, and I'm going to give it some thought.

It's ludicrous to "replace" columns anyway. Once a column appears in the paper, it's gone. "Now it belongs to the ages." It's out there. You can replace it in the archives, but people have already read it. Already laughed or cried or recoiled in horror. Junkies have already saved it to their hard drives. You can't replace a column. You can only replace a columnist. Wait — strike that.

Finally, let me address the proposed $27,500 price tag for replacement of Town Hall columns. This seems high. From the beginning, I have written "The Outsidah" column on a strictly volunteer basis. You don't have to offer me $27,500 to stop writing rotten things about Town Hall or about insects. Even if all the *Ipswich Chronicle*'s columnists divvy up the $27,500, this is still a lot of money — more money than the typical columnist ever sees at one time.

No one from Town Hall has consulted me about how much money I would need to make an adjustment in my Town Hall columns. If a selectman had casually dropped by my house, ostensibly just to say hello, but then nonchalantly slipped a couple hundred-dollar bills into my pocket, and then if said selectman had mentioned, with something of a chuckle, that I needed to lay off writing about Town Hall, I would have felt more than adequately induced. I don't need a line item in the Town's capital budget, and I certainly don't need to be an Article at Town Meeting. I am happy to stop writing rot about Town Hall at the drop of a bribe.

It will be harder to give up writing about insects, though. I love to hate those little guys.

Welcome to our town!

Three views of an Ipswich institution...

I think our town-wide New Year's

resolution should be to change all the street names that aren't really accurate.

For example: When you turn at the ClamBox and head toward Linebrook Road, you think you're on Mile Lane — but this is a lie. You're on a lane that only lasts for eight-tenths of a mile. If you try to go a mile on Mile Lane, you'll wind up in Mrs. Wallenfinch's backyard. She has rhubarb growing out there, and the ground is soft, and you'll find yourself up to your axles, sputtering and cursing and dialing Skillman's on your cell phone to pull you out of the muck. All because a street was misnamed.

Short Street is short, but Middle Road, on Little Neck, is actually off-center. School Street takes you to the school, but Cleveland Avenue gets you no place close to Cleveland.

Central Street is pretty central. Pleasant Street is pleasant enough. Barnside Drive truly lets you drive alongside a barn. And yeah, most of the year, I gotta say, Brown Square is pretty brown. But Circle Drive is actually a slightly wiggly line. You can follow Topsfield Road to get to Topsfield, and Essex Street to get to Essex — but can you take High Street to get high?

Is Congress Street dysfunctional?

Some previous street-naming errors appear to have been corrected. In the old days, Ipswich had a street called Gravel. Then, apparently, they paved it; it couldn't really be called Gravel anymore. So they renamed it Liberty Street. Very nice. A lofty concept. But then they made it one-way, so it empties out at Lord's Square — which is more or less impossible. So this poor street has ended up misnamed yet again. To be accurate, we should call it Stuck Street. Or maybe Standstill Station?

I feel wistful about some of the name changes. Back in the day, Meadowview Lane was known as Three Sisters Circle. This is a lovely name for a street. The three sisters must have made some serious enemies in this town, though, to be expunged like this, smudged into a generic subdivision designation like Meadowview Lane.

Likewise, we have First and Second Streets, and then we have Fourth, Fifth, and Sixth Streets — but somebody must have done something really bad on Third Street, because it's been obliterated.

Leslie Road used to be Tobacco Pipe Hill Road. Maybe people got tired of those big SMOKING CAUSES LUNG CANCER signs the feds insisted on.

It seems at some point Ipswich went through a doleful period. Heartbreak Road — now there's a sad name. Labor in Vain: Who decided on this? Sure, I have bad days once in a while, but I can't imagine getting discouraged enough to say, "Let's call it Shoot Me Now Street."

And one can only imagine the unfortunate marriage that led to the naming of Nags Head Road. I hope the poor fellow somehow managed to get to Paradise Road.

BUTTER IS GOOD FOR YOU

The holidays are well behind us, and

I do mean well.

2012 will go down in history as the year of the Great Butter Crisis.

It began when we learned that an old friend from Arizona, a great lover of lobster — trapped in a life just about as far from the lobsters as you can possibly get — would visit us for Thanksgiving. Great lobster enthusiasts ourselves, we determined that our Thanksgiving dinner would feature turkey of the sea: six big lobsters from Captain Joe's, on the dock in Gloucester. We like to get lobsters from Joe's because it's fun to buy them off the boats, but of course you can get lobsters just about anywhere these days. There was such a glut of lobsters this season that prices sank to near-record lows, and lobster tanks were appearing everywhere from Market Basket to Toys R Us. When the Y complained to the Board of Selectmen that their water bill had mysteriously shot up, I immediately suspected them of secretly operating a hidden lobster tank connected underground to the swimming pool. No charges have yet been filed.

So I procured the doomed animals on the day before

Thanksgiving, and stuck them in a big plastic bag in the fridge — which I'm sure for a lobster is like a small vacation villa in an exotic faraway location. Come cooking time on Thanksgiving Day, we pulled them out, snipped their rubber bracelets, and without a single qualm, boiled them blazing red.

But then, of course, with lobsters, you need butter.

Discovering on Thanksgiving Day that you need butter can be marriage-threatening. Recriminations abound. Spouses may momentarily forget their manners. And someone — in this case, the husband — has to go find some butter.

Mumbling bad words, I drove an entire eight-tenths of a mile to the Cumberland Farms convenience store on Route 1, and stalked straight back to the dairy section.

There was no butter.

It was Thanksgiving Day, of course, and lots of people were using butter.

There was margarine, but in our household, buying margarine would be more marriage-threatening than forgetting to buy butter.

So I headed down Linebrook Road to the Central Street Cumby's.

As the employees watched me heading for the dairy case, they seemed to shrivel a bit, in exhaustion and despair.

There was no butter

there, either. "People have been coming in for butter all day long," one worker said. Then she tried to brighten a little: "We're going to get some on Monday!"

It was for moments like this that someone invented the word *Grrrrr.*

I was not about to traipse all the way to the Topsfield Cumby's only to discover they had no butter. Growling to myself, I pulled out my trusty iPhone and tracked down their phone number.

"Do you have any butter?"

I heard what surely sounded like the hysterical laughter of the insane.

"Sir, we not only have no butter, we have no heavy cream, no whipped cream, no milk, no Half & Half, and yes, we have no bananas." You know when a Cumby's manager quotes a 1922 show tune, he is close to, or possibly already over, the edge.

So — bottom line — what we managed to achieve here in Ipswich, on Thanksgiving Day 2012, was a kind of perfect storm: the deadly coming-together of high-fat diet and poor planning. I for one intend to see to it that nothing like the Great Butter Crisis happens again — and not by any change of diet. Butter will appear on every Brendel family grocery list, no matter how much we already have on hand. If necessary, we will store the excess outside in the snow. God did not intend lobsters to be eaten with margarine, nor to appear in court records as grounds for divorce.

YOUR RAVE HERE

The biggest-selling English-language
newspaper in the world is not, as some believe, the *Ipswich Chronicle*. Nor even the *Salem News*. It's the *Times of India*. Every single day, 3.14 million copies of the *Times of India* are consumed, edging out the *Ipswich Chronicle* by a substantial margin.

The *Times of India*'s owners, two brothers, make no

pretense of being journalists, or even caring about journalism. Without apology, they run the paper as a money-making business, plain and simple. There's little or no investigative journalism, nothing remotely like the *Ipswich Chronicle*'s crack reporting on Caldwell condo conversion complaints or its exposé of unclaimed checks at Town Hall. Instead, the *Times of India* is simply an enormous bulletin board — information about "what happened yesterday" — and a colossal overabundance of advertisements. Many of the "news articles" are actually paid for by people or organizations who want coverage in the *Times of India*. In fact, for $450,000, you can literally buy the entire front page of the paper, masthead and all — even rename the newspaper for that day if you want.

Prissy American journalists are horrified by this approach to the newspaper business — we primly insist on keeping our newsrooms separate and distinct from the "business side" — but the *Times of India* is thriving, unlike hundreds of U.S. papers, and its owners are millionaires many times over.

I say, Ipswich, let's learn from success.

My recommendations, for purposes of getting discussion under way, are as follows:

• For $125, a *Chronicle* reporter will write a front-page article about how your Ipswich church is better than all the other Ipswich churches because it bans fewer of the really good sins.

• A mini-auction will determine whether ClamBox, Clambake, or Clam House gets the most glowing review. The bidding starts at $250. For an additional $100, we'll trash the other two places. For $125 more, we'll throw in a fake botulism scare.

• $17.50 a week turns the "Ipswich Watchdogs"

Facebook page into an actual page of the paper. Hottest topics, like sale of the old Rec. Department air hockey table, may require more than one page, and a surcharge. Or else some discreet censorship.

- The School Committee can pay 1% of the Feoffees funds to get a weekly comic strip about the Feoffees. It would have cute little New Feoffees and adorable little Old Feoffees, and they would always be getting into amusing little conflicts, and Laura Dietz would always come in at the end to resolve the problem wisely, but of course she never gets appreciated for it, yet she still retains her grace and good humor, and bravely comes back for more in next week's strip.
- For a mere $20 a week, Al Boynton gets a photo feature — alternating weekly between tragic shots of the deterioration of Old Town Hall's historical value and pictures of his dog.
- We'll take $35 to run an article every week, year-round, about the Ipswich football cheerleading squad getting ready for Nationals.
- It will take $45 to say something good about the Whittier Motel expansion, or something bad about the Town's wind turbines; $10 discount for both. For an additional $15, we'll avoid mentioning the North Main streetscape improvement project altogether.
- For an extra $3 a week, you get a special edition of the paper that includes people's names in the Police Log.
- And finally, I'll personally be contributing $10 a week to run the name, address, phone, and Social Security number of every driver who does 40 on the 25-mph section of Linebrook Road.

Of course these are only idea-starters. I think you can see the financial possibilities. As the *Times of India* proves, a great newspaper isn't all about great journalism. There's something to be said for buying good will, too. And facilitating personal vendettas.

Let's get started!

Welcome to our town!

Drive up through Ipswich on 133-1A, and you'll come away with at least three significant visual memories....

Come again!

PASSAGE TO INFAMY

This is about a friend of mine, who

shall remain nameless, and who, like me, hasn't lived in
Ipswich long, and who, like me, lives in an antique house,
one of those quirky places added to, revised, and
generally cobbled together over the centuries in such a
way that the resulting residence is something like the

interior of an old lady's handbag. A monument to perplexity. Why does this nook lead to that cranny? How can all the kitchen doors be too narrow to get this fridge in or out?

In this particular house, you had to traipse through a bathroom to get from one side of the house to the other. You can imagine the awkward moments. If someone is, shall we say, using the facilities, you can't really go in. You're trapped, either in the front of the house, or the rear. Of course you can wait for the, uh, user to finish, ahem, using. If you're short on time, however, your options are limited. Even if it's only someone in the shower, and you open the bathroom door very, very quietly and try to tiptoe through, it's possible that you'll suddenly get to know the person taking the shower a bit more intimately than either of you would have preferred at that moment.

Your other option is to go outside, walk around the house, and come back in on the other side. This option is particularly unpleasant when your sardonic neighbor, noticing you from the adjacent property, won't leave it alone. "How's it goin', Larry? Betsy's in the shower, eh?" Also: Take your key. It's awkward enough to be seen stalking around your own house, out one door and in the other, but it's humiliating to arrive at your destination, find yourself locked out, and have no choice but to go back and do it all over again. "How's it goin', Larry? Locked out with Betsy in the shower, eh?" Not that I've ever experienced this myself, you understand.

So my friend, handyman that he is, employed a simple but ingenious solution. He cut off one edge of the bathroom by erecting a new wall, complete with door, forming a convenient corridor. You no longer have to interrupt whatever someone's doing in the bathroom (I hesitate to be more specific) in order to cross from the front of the house to the back. Which is a huge relief. Not that I've ever experienced this relief personally, you understand. We're talking about my friend's house.

The new hallway is attractive: it's painted, it has baseboards and crown molding and ample lighting. And the new wall is sturdy. If you happen to stumble in that hallway — I'm not speculating as to why you might be stumbling, but let's just say you stumble — this new wall will hold you up. Not that I've tried it out, mind you. But I can say on good authority that even after an inordinate number of martinis, or if you lose your balance because that third floorboard is somewhat wobbly and sometimes takes you by surprise — no matter how or why you fall down like a fool and crash against the new wall — you cannot knock this wall down.

It may, however, have to come down.

A longtime Ipswich resident happened to be visiting recently.

"Look at the new wall I built!"

The friend looked the new wall up and down, frowning.

"You get a permit for this?"

"Huh?"

As it turns out, there are some 2,114 pages of building code in the Commonwealth of Massachusetts, and an additional 189 pages or so just for Ipswich; and as any longtime Ipswich resident knows, every paragraph of these regulations must be consulted, every detail of a project approved, before anything gets built in Ipswich. The Town of Ipswich Building Department's own website actually lays it on the line: "Anything other than paint and paper will probably require a Building Permit."

Who knew?

However, it's probably not feasible to tear down the wall and do it all over again legally. Simpler to pay the friend to keep quiet.

To keep up with the hush-money payments, a collection box has been installed in the illegal hallway. Every time you cross from one end of the house to the other, you put in a dollar. And thank God He's protected you from Inspector Sperber for one more day.

Please don't tell.

THE OFFICIAL IPSWICH LIST

I haven't lived in Ipswich long. (You

have to keep saying this for your first 20 years here; then you can switch to "I realize I'm not a native." After a total of 45 years, you're allowed to avoid the issue, unless a townie challenges you to confess.)

But I want to be a good New Englander and learn about uniquely New Englandish things. So I have set out to learn all the official Massachusetts stuff.

And of course, since this is New England, it's complicated.

The state bird is the black-capped chickadee. Not just any chickadee. It has to have a black cap. Why? I don't know. Perhaps this is information they only give you after you've lived here 20 years.

But there's not only a state bird; there's also a state *game* bird, which is the wild turkey. Not just any turkey. It has to be wild. Docile, well-behaved turkeys, turkeys that do their homework and avoid loud parties and graduate on time, are not recognized by the Commonwealth. A turkey from UMass-Amherst would be a shoo-in for state game bird.

There's also a state dog — the Boston terrier, which makes sense — and a state fish: the cod — no surprise there either. There's even a state insect: the ladybug.

There does not, however, seem to be official Ipswich stuff. I would like to be a good, constructive citizen, so I've decided to suggest some official Ipswich stuff.

For example, our town bird should be the crow. (The crows in my yard are so big, when they demanded I suggest them for town bird, I was afraid to say no.) For town game bird, we could designate the hawk that ate two of my neighbor's chickens last year. The official Ipswich dog should be Al Boynton's dog Sobe, simply because this is the most-photographed dog in the history of Facebook. The official Ipswich fish (try saying *that* five times fast) could be ClamBox haddock. Our Ipswich insect would of course be the greenhead. I suggest altering the official town seal, also, to include a depiction of the official town insect with a dagger plunged through its evil little heart.

The state cat is the tabby; the town cat would be the fisher. No, it's not actually a cat, but it's *perfect* for Ipswich. Massachusetts has a state shell: the New England Neptune. Our official Ipswich shell would be the clam. Natch.

The state marine mammal is the right whale. The Ipswich marine mammal will be any number of individuals spotted on a summer day at Crane Beach.

The state flower is the mayflower, of course. I think

the town flower should be the cheap plastic bouquet in the imitation gold vase that I gave the new Town Manager when she first got here.

Massachusetts has an official state fossil: the theropod (T. Rex was one of these guys). Ipswich will need an official town fossil. I hesitate to name just one.

The official state gem is rhodonite. The official town gem, in my opinion, is Dorothy Monnelly. A photographer-artist extraordinaire, and a lovely friend.

Official state rock: Roxbury puddingstone. This is what you find under foot in Boston and 11 other cities and towns. Our official Ipswich rock should be the granite boulder that I broke my back digging out of my backyard.

Our official state folk hero is Johnny Appleseed, who went around planting apple trees. For Ipswich, we should have Johnny Clamseed, who goes around seeding clam beds. State heroine: Deborah Samson, who posed as a man and fought in the War of Independence. Ipswich heroine: Kristina Brendel, who posed as a gallery director and fought in the Business Owners' Wars until there was no money left. I am a witness.

Massachusetts has a state folk dance: the square dance. The official Ipswich town dance would be the "Town Meeting tap dance" — which is whatever the person onstage does when they can't answer the question from the person at the mic.

State beverage: cranberry juice. Town beverage: Ipswich ale. A no-brainer. State dessert: Boston cream pie. Town dessert: whatever Christopher's Table is serving tonight.

Our official Massachusetts state cookie is the chocolate chip. Our official Ipswich town cookie should be — aw, you can't beat chocolate chip.

LET IT SNOW, I AIN'T AFRAID

I looked out Friday evening at

Winter Storm Nemo dropping tons of snow on my driveway, and I said to myself, "Gosh, that's going to take my wife a long time to shovel."

On Saturday I came to my senses, and headed out to do the honorable thing, leaving her inside to sweep, mop, dust, wash, iron, and paint the bedroom. The bedroom did not really need painting, but it's irresistible to do those few things that the Town of Ipswich doesn't require a permit for.

Of course, I was well-equipped for my snow removal chores. When I moved here from the Arizona desert, where we saw exactly 16 flakes of snow in two decades (and those 16 flakes came in two separate "snowstorms"), I knew I would need the proper equipment. So I bought a snowblower. Not just any snowblower. I bought a tiny electric snowblower. Essentially a large metal mosquito. Because I have no experience with snowblowers, and I wanted one I could handle. I could imagine nothing more embarrassing than running down Linebrook Road chasing my snowblower. I have seen big snowblowers in my neighborhood. Snowblowers bigger than the facial-hairy, barrel-chested lumberjack-types who drive them. Snowblowers bigger than the sheds they're stored in. Snowblowers so big, they clear the average Linebrook driveway just by being powered up, and only need to be operated longer because their motors shake the earth and knock another ton of snow out of the trees. This kind of snowblower — the kind of snowblower the Old Testament Goliath would have owned, if he were from Gloucester instead of Gath, the gas hog snowblower, the snowblower you could pull a house trailer with — was not for me. I needed a starter-snowblower. A kindergartener's snowblower. A snowblower as delicate and sweet-tempered and unobtrusive as its owner.

When the garage door went up, Nemo's drifts remained in place, a solid wall of snow, significantly taller than my snowblower. At first I decided I would have to use my shovel. But within a minute or two, my thoracolumbar fascia muscle had conferred with my trapezius muscle and confirmed that my back had been too many weeks without anything remotely like exercise to take on something the size of Nemo.

So I took a deep breath and pushed my little snowsneezer into the mammoth mountain of white.

I was surprised to see how well the tiny Toro performed. It chewed up the bottom two or three inches of snow, leaving a two-and-a-half foot ledge of snow above it. I could keep pushing the machine into the snow bank, bit by bit, deeper and deeper, until the overhanging ledge got too heavy and weak, and crashed down, leaving me fresh snow to blow. In this way, a few inches at a time, I made my way from the door of my house toward Linebrook Road.

Visibility was an issue, however. I couldn't really see where I was heading. When I finally climbed up from the depths to figure out my location, there was a sign that said Topsfield Town Line.

Returning along the trail I'd blazed with my marvelous little machine, I found that my very excellent neighbor, who owns a snowblower twice the size of his boat, had graciously cleared my entire property. The driveway, the yard, the garden, everything. Everything except the igloo.

Well, it looked like an igloo. It was actually my Honda. An Ipswich tax collector was standing nearby with a clipboard.

"We don't seem to have a record of this dwelling," he said peevishly. "Your property tax will be going up."

"It's my Honda!" I replied. "Honest!"

"Well, then, it's a garage," he snorted, jotting notes. "Did you get a permit to build this?"

One of the many things I love about

Ipswich is that we're safe here. Safe enough that my neighbor, who is a Lawrence cop, makes fun of how safe Ipswich is. Ipswich is so safe that it's becoming a kind of haven for law enforcement officials. Where does the chief of police for the city of Gloucester live? In Ipswich. If you spend all day dealing with crime and criminals, the last thing you want when you go home at the end of the day is to deal with more crime and more criminals. So you move to Ipswich.

I think we're all pretty safe here in Ipswich, but I happen to be extra-safe. From my backyard I could throw a rock and hit not only the Lawrence cop, but also a Lynnfield firefighter, a Salem firefighter, and a Massachusetts state trooper. Of course I would not throw said rock, because it's so embarrassing to be arrested by your own neighbor.

"This your rock, buddy?"

"Kevin! It was a joke!"

"You nailed my chihuahua. Assault and battery."

"Kevin! It's me! Your pal from two doors down!"

"Hands behind your back, please. I'm gonna hafta cuff ya."

When my wife and I had the opportunity to move, to live anywhere we wanted in the whole wide world, to relocate permanently and spend the rest of our lives somewhere, we chose Ipswich. We'd had our fill of the big city, the master-planned community, the Disneyesque suburbs. We longed for small-town America. I've lived in Chicago (three times as deadly as New York City). I've lived in Phoenix (17th most dangerous metro area in the country, according to the annual Morgan Quitno study). I've lived in Akron, Ohio. (They have almost twice the violent crime rate of the national average, says CityRating.com — fewer than 200,000 people, but more than 20 murders a year. Shrinking tax base? Hey! Cut down on your murders! You'll have more taxpayers left!)

Ipswich was perfect. The ocean, the history, the clams. Good schools for our brilliant kid, good vibe overall. And a low crime rate — officially safer than 63% of all U.S. cities. Sure, there's the occasional crazy who sticks up the convenience store, but these aren't our people. These people come in from neighboring towns (which shall remain nameless) and can easily be barred if we impose the simple electric-fence plan I've recommended to the Town Manager.

To find out how Ipswich got to be so safe, I made a date with Chief Paul Nikas. He took me on a tour of the Elm Street police station — a building most locals know only from the outside. Inside this aging structure, the Chief and his minions have created an impressive, up-to-date operation. There's a super-fast digital fingerprint-matching machine. A big, intimidating, multi-screen security station and 911 center. Of course, there are also the homey touches you'd expect in a small-town police station: the police team bowling trophy. The popcorn machine. Old records kept in beer boxes. (If you broke the law here in 1966, you're in the Pabst Blue Ribbon crate. Schlitz is '69.)

But the secret weapon — clearly the key reason Ipswich is so safe — is that the jail cells are pink. Not pinkish. Not something that sort of reminds you of pink. These walls are absolutely, totally pink. It's the same princess pink that your elementary-school daughter wants in her bedroom.

When a hardened criminal gets locked up in one of these cells, he recoils in horror at the cuteness of it. He shivers and squeezes his eyes closed. He vows to himself to go straight. Or at least, next time, to rob a store in Rowley instead.

I'm tellin' ya, Chief Nikas is a crime-fighting *genius*.

My math whiz fifth-grader calculates

that, in the short time we've lived in Ipswich, I've driven Linebrook Road the equivalent of driving cross-country and back: about 6,846 miles.

Indeed, it seems to me that driving across Ipswich is kind of like driving across the United States. If you know your U.S. geography, you might agree that our town is sort of a 42-square-mile microcosm of the entire country. Consider:

- I live in outer Linebrook, that mysterious triangle beyond Route 1, so we're the West Coasters of Ipswich. "Outer Linebrook" sounds like a forgotten planet, and many folks think of California the same way. And like our Hollywood brethren, we outer Linebrookians loll about in our sunglasses and bathing suits and eat vegetarian and refer to our part of town as "West Ipswich Farms."

- The Pacific Northwest of Ipswich is out toward the end of High Street. By the time you reach White Farms Ice Cream, you're perilously close to the Rowley line — just like when you get to Seattle, you're almost in Russia. (Well, you do have to go through Sarah Palin's house, but *then* you're almost in Russia.) Sad to say, however, even though Seattle is a great fish town, at Sal's Pizza, next door to White Farms, there's not a single anchovy on the menu.

- To find Ipswich's answer to the Upper Midwest, you go straight up Town Farm Road. The further you go, the more Minnesota it gets. "The Land of 10,000 Lakes" has nothing on the Ipswich Transfer Station — our own "Land of 10,000 Recycled Car Batteries."

Minnesota, one of the greenest states in the Union, would applaud our fine facility, where you can recycle everything from paint to poison, fluorescent bulbs to forsythia branches.

- Our Northeast is the Necks: Jeffreys, Great, and Little. Especially Little. Here we find our Pilgrims (staked their claim!), our Puritans (righteous to the end!), and our colonists (who, in the time-tested tradition of John Winthrop, Jr., buy off the natives, take legal control of the land, and henceforth call themselves "natives"). The rest of the country thinks of the Northeast as flinty — stern and unemotional and strict with every nickel. The rest of the town thinks of Little Neck as — hm, sorry, I can't seem to read my notes here. Let's move on.

- Follow Topsfield Road through our own Ipswich version of the Great Southwest. Winding up in the Willowdale State Forest, however, is infinitely more pleasant than winding up in the sizzling Sonora Desert. As a longtime resident of the sizzling Sonora Desert, I know whereof I speak.

- To get to our Deep South, follow County to Lakemans to Fellows to Candlewood: You'll find people sitting barefoot in creaky rocking chairs on half-rotted front porches drinking moonshine from clay jugs and spitting tobacco juice through their remaining teeth at their rusted '57 trucks up on blocks in their front yards. Well, not all of them. Just my friends who live there. (You know who you are.)

- In the U.S., you go as far as you can to the southeast and you wind up in Florida. In Ipswich, you follow 133 southeast as far as you can, and you wind up at the Great Marsh — our answer to the Everglades.

- And if you follow the interstate from the heart of our nation to the east coast, you come to Washington, D.C., the center of power. In Ipswich, you follow Argilla Road from the center of town to the east, and you come to the Crane Estate, historic destination of the great and near-great. President Taft partied here. To get from my humble abode to the Great House on Castle Hill is a 9.4-mile journey. It takes 23 minutes in my automobile, unless someone ahead of me on Central decides to be nice and gives someone on Market the right-of-way, in which case the ensuing traffic tangle — vehicles on North Main, South Main, Central, and Market trapped in a slow-motion tango of you-go-first gesticulation — will turn my 23 minutes into 42. Almost quicker to drive cross-country.

  Just kidding. I love it here.

LET IT BLOW, LET IT BLOW, LET IT BLOW

This Monday was the "Invention

Convention" at Doyon Elementary School, and the fifth-graders inspired me. With kids creating contraptions to crack all kinds of conflicts, and mountains of old snow stacked all around Ipswich, I had an epiphany: When it comes to snow and snow removal, we need to think more ... *inventively*.

We don't need a more ergonomically efficient shovel, or a more massive gas-guzzling snowblower.

What we need is heat.

We know how to make heat. We started making heat back when cavemen figured out fire. There's a blow dryer hanging on a peg in my bathroom that can burn hairs down to the follicle in less time than it takes to floss your teeth. I am a witness. So why not forget about funneling all that energy into snow-blowing, and concentrate instead on snow-scorching? Snow-warming. Snow-melting.

We have the technology. I'm proposing an enormous blow dryer: the SnowTorch™ — a state-of-the-art snow-torching machine. (To test the prototype, I nominate my impressive snowblowing hero of a neighbor — not me, because I don't do well with heavy equipment, even an electric razor.) The SnowTorch™ is deceptively simple: the same machinery as your common everyday ordinary bathroom blow dryer, but scaled up. Massively scaled up. Just flip the switch, the fan roars, the hot air blasts out of the barrel, and the snow starts to melt.

Yes, there will be a lot of melting, and it will happen quickly. None of this 90-day slow-melt plan that New England seems to be on. The SnowTorch™ will generate a floodtide of snowmelt, flowing downhill, turning Linebrook Road into the Linebrook River, or at least the Linebrook Brook, and splashing out onto Route 1 at Cumby's. But have no fear. If we can torch-and-scorch our snow by adapting blow dryer technology, we can dry up the subsequent snowmelt by adapting your dentist's spray-sucking technology. I'm talking about that little tube that the beautiful assistant sticks into your mouth to suck out all the water that the dentist is spraying into your mouth to distract you from the screaming of the drill.

So here's the plan. You rev up your SnowTorch™, concentrating the astonishing blast of hot air onto the snow on your driveway, but then there's also this snakelike contraption lying off to one side, on the downhill side. It's your VacuMelt™, a huge snakelike contraption, and it's sucking the meltage off the pavement as fast as the SnowTorch™ can produce it. In a few minutes, your driveway is not only snow-free, it's perfectly dry. (No more of the classic New England melt-by-day, freeze-by-night, fall-on-your-butt-on-the-way-to-the-mailbox syndrome.)

And where does your VacuMelt™ put all that water? Good news. The same technology that gave us the teapot will be adapted to create the SteamStream™. The water goes in, gets super-heated super-fast, and streams out a spout (whistle optional) into the air. The dry winter air moistens pleasurably. People start planting tropical flowers in their yards. Those sad, dirty snow banks lining your street and obstructing your visibility? Gone — replaced by banks of orchids and calla lilies.

Or you can buy an adapter that lets you point your SteamStream™ into your mudroom, and turn it into a sauna. People will start looking forward to winter, and maybe even sigh wistfully as they finally roll their SnowTorch™ into the garage in the spring.

SnowTorch™, VacuMelt™, SteamStream™. I'm on it. As soon as that government grant comes through.

IPSWICH EXPLAINS EVERYTHING

There is a God, and here is how I
know.

I was driving my very small car on 1A, northbound toward Ipswich center. There's that certain place, at the north end of the South Green, where the road swings to the left, and becomes South Main Street. I so swung.

But if you're coming the opposite direction, *from* Ipswich center, on South Main, the road splits. You can keep bending to the right, if you want to stay on 1A and head south toward the Whittier, or Hamilton. Or, you can keep going straight, onto a tiny little stretch of asphalt that soon leads you to a stop sign, and then deposits you on Poplar Street.

The deadly problem is this: Do you realize, as you're approaching this fork in the road, that if you go straight, toward Poplar, you're actually crossing traffic? It's true. If you bend to the right and head south on 1A, you're safe. But what if you actually go straight — the way that "feels right" if you're not from around here? The cars coming up from the south on 1A are barreling toward you with no reason to stop. No warning that you're going straight, pretty as you please, unwittingly crossing traffic as you do so.

So here I am, in my very small car, heading north on 1A, beautifully bending to the west at the north end of the South Green, when I find a very large car heading east on South Main, and very definitely *not* taking the curve to stay on 1A. This fellow is going straight — toward Poplar Street — crossing traffic without realizing it. Pretty as you please.

In that split second before you die, your automatic HD-vision kicks in. I could see, in that moment of helplessness and anguish, this was a gray 2009 Toyota Sequoia SUV with a triangle of rust on the front left bumper, where perhaps a telephone pole had interfered with the vehicle's progress on a snowy night a couple years ago. I could see that the driver was a slightly overweight young man with an inferior haircut, perfectly in style, and by the gleam in his eye I would say he was trying to impress his even younger girlfriend, a pretty brunette seated on the passenger side, exactly where I was about to make contact, in a most unpleasant way.

Theoretically, the SUV was going 25 mph maximum, because who would have the nerve to speed in such close proximity to the Ipswich police station on Elm Street? And theoretically, I was going 25 mph maximum, because I am a model citizen. The impact of two vehicles colliding at 25 mph can be calculated by the simple equation we all remember from high school math class, right? Kinetic energy is equal to one-half the mass times the velocity squared. To put it another way: This is going to be a huge mess.

There was no way the boy could stop his SUV in time. There was no way I could stop my very small car in time. This is where God comes in. The boy's car screeched and swerved. My car swerved and screeched. In a magical moment, the boy driver and I looked into each other's eyes, and both of us saw stupidity.

It is clear to me that there is a God. The Town of Ipswich proves it. God lives and works on the north end of the South Green, where 1A curves away from Poplar Street. The Town of Ipswich also explains why there is suffering in the world. There is suffering in the world because God is busy elsewhere. He is largely consumed with preventing crashes on the north end of the South Green, where 1A curves away from Poplar Street.

It is a privilege to live here. It would be remarkable enough for the question of God's existence to be settled by a small town in New England. Or for the question of why there is suffering in the world to be settled by a small town in New England. But for both questions to be settled by the *same* small town in New England is really something.

Ipswich, I salute you. Er, us. Whatever. I'm still rattled by that near miss.

ROWLEY: WHAT'S NOT TO LOVE?

I hardly know where to begin.

The shock, the shame, the sheer agony of the situation has left me — me, the loquacious one, the wordy guy — nearly speechless.

As you read these words, I am fewer than 100 hours away from becoming the owner of a business in (I can hardly type the word without shaking my head in amazement) Rowley.

After years of mercilessly using the Town of Rowley as the butt of innumerable jokes in this very column, after deflecting well-deserved barbs via email from incensed Rowley residents, after surviving what I still believe to be a poisoning attempt in a Rowley dining room following publication of a particularly snarky column, after sanctimoniously announcing my vow to forego Rowley put-downs in print, only to fall off the wagon a few brief weeks later — after all of this and more, as fate would have it, I will soon have a Rowley business address.

Coincidence? Or cosmic justice?

My ironic mock-Shakespearean tragedy unfolded as follows.

Wife Kristina directed Time & Tide Fine Art on Market Street in Ipswich for two-and-a-half years. Great vibe, fun events, brilliant artists — but we bled money: good sales per shopper, but too few shoppers downtown. Kristina announced the closing three days after Christmas. Lots of people in Ipswich expressed their grief. I was one of them. (It should be pointed out, however, that not a single Rowley resident sent a message along the lines of "Serves you right, scum," nor even "Neener neener neener.")

Soon Kristina heard from a Rowley business, Post Road Framers. They had always operated a gallery in the front of their shop, near Market Basket on Route 1. Would Time & Tide like to move in? Without asking me — and I hasten to point this out, because if this turns out badly, I would like to avoid as much blame as possible — Kristina negotiated a workable agreement, and agreed.

Time & Tide will reopen in Rowley, Massachusetts, on April 1. That's April Fools Day, by the way.

She will throw a "grand opening" reception on Saturday, April 6 (from 5 to 7 p.m.), and I'll be there. You're invited. Whether I'll be wearing a bullet-proof vest is not a subject I feel comfortable discussing publicly.

For my fellow Ipswich residents who intend to venture out for the party, let me offer a few words of gentle advice.

1. Contrary to a common misunderstanding, you do not need to carry your passport. The border between Ipswich and Rowley is open.

2. When you pass the turnoff for the Ipswich Country Club, breathe deeply. If you feel lightheaded, breathe in through your nose and out through your mouth. What you're experiencing is the heady delight of sensible zoning and permitting, two of Rowley's most desirable distinctives.

3. After crossing the border into Rowley, continue driving normally. Traffic rules in Rowley are very similar to those in Ipswich. Do not be alarmed by people driving various speeds. Your natural Ipswichian inclination to go 40 mph no matter the speed limit will dissipate gradually after you've been in Rowley awhile. Rowley drivers are known to acknowledge speed limit signs. These are white rectangular signs with black numerals, which normally go unnoticed in Ipswich.

4. When exiting your vehicle, continue to behave as you would in Ipswich. Do not look around nervously for "the torch and pitchfork people," in the words of my friend Tim, who lives across from Rowley Town Hall. You will find the citizens of Rowley to be nearly indistinguishable from citizens of Ipswich. On close examination, however, you may find that their skin is somewhat smoother: fewer wrinkles from scowling and fewer scars from local battles. This is because, for the most part, they still cling to that old-fashioned notion of civil discourse.

Got the looks, got the hair, and he

plays the guitar
And he's loved by each starlet and diva
He's oozing with talent, he's a megawatt star
And a hard-working over-achieva

Got a fabulous house, got a view of the bay
Got a life which there is none superber
Got his musical gigs, got his groupies, and hey
Gets to work every day with Jim Sperber

Oh Lord, I do pray
Somehow you'll agree
And just for one day
Oh please, let me be Eric Colville

On YouTube he gets shocking numbers of hits
And he's got those awards for songwriting
I stare just as long as politeness permits
Knowing I'll never be that exciting

Oh Lord, hear my prayer
It comes from the heart
I know you are there
And how great Thou art

Oh Lord, I do pray
Somehow you'll agree
And just for one day
Oh please, let me be Eric Colville

When he steps from his mystery space on South Main
With a grace and a charm I will never attain
As he strides across Five Corners, grooving his groove
You can feel all of Ipswich improve

As a structural engineer, he is a star
Builders outside of Ipswich affirm it
He's as great at the code as he is at guitar
And to prove it, he'll hold up your permit

Oh Lord, I do pray
Somehow you'll agree
And just for one day
Oh please, let me be
Eric Colville
Eric Colville

You can find Doug's very bad musical version of "Please Let Me Be" at YouTube.com/user/dougbrendel. Find the much better music of Ipswich's assistant building inspector at EricColville.com.

Now, finally, after all those false

starts, those maddeningly mild days in February, those sadistically sunny days in March, now, finally, we can perhaps look back on winter, and assess.

I have not lived in New England very long, so perhaps my powers of assessment are limited, compared to the over-arching wisdom of locals, townies, long-termers, lifers, and the smart-looking gray-haired woman in the checkout line ahead of me yesterday, who I overheard admitting somewhat shame-facedly that she had only lived here 29 years, so what did she know.

But in spite of my greenness, let me boldly say, my take on the winter we've just emerged from is as follows: Pretty good.

Times I skidded my very small car into a snowbank: Zero. (Times I thanked God for a near miss: 119.)

Times I heard a native New Englander say, "I love the snow": Zero.

Times a middle schooler playing hockey on the frozen pond south of Linebrook Road across from Howe Street was trapped in the ice and extricated only by heavy-duty machinery brought in from Topsfield: Zero.

Times I fell on the ice and broke my neck: Zero. (Times I slipped and wrenched my back but caught myself before I splattered on the cruel crust of New England and required an ambulance: 14.)

Number of deer found warming their hooves on warm bags of garbage recently set out behind the ClamBox: Zero.

Times the power went out, leaving us huddled around our fireplace, wishing we had thought ahead to buy a generator, a camp stove, anything: Zero. (Why? Because last spring, I bought a generator, and a camp stove.)

Times I had to burrow through the snow to get to my mailbox, only to find my mailman immobile in his vehicle, his body a grotesque ice sculpture, unnaturally bent halfway between his sorting box, his lips snarled into the shape of "Why the devil do these people need all these catalogs?", and my mailbox, where he would have reached out to touch the fiendishly cold door-handle and instantly become a pillar of ice, if only his body had still been liquid enough to reach out at all: Zero.

Times the desperately frigid temperatures drove Ipswich citizens thrashing out local issues online to temporarily suspend the warfare and devote themselves to shoveling their driveways: Zero.

Times I peeked out my front window to see if my neighbor across the street was using his enormous snowblower and wondered if he might come help me with my driveway: 147.

Times I told my fifth-grader, "Wear a coat": Zero. (Why? Because she began training me four years ago, when she was a first-grader, that children do not require coats.)

Number of inches the snowbank at the corner of Linebrook and Randall Road exceeded the height of my very small car: 17.

Times I thanked God for those Ipswich get-up-in-the-middle-of-the-night road-scraper guys: 1,147,248. We don't appreciate them enough.

Yes, this winter, we lost some good friends. Some old friends. Every winter, in its way, is a rough winter. And we had some disagreements. Some stuff is just a matter of taste. Of preference. A difference of opinion.

But it was a good winter. A New England winter. We weathered it. We are still together.

Love conquers all.

Dear Outsidah,

First I have to say (the note began), the *Chronicle* humiliated me. "The first call came in at 3:19 a.m. Friday," they said, "and the last call, so far, came in at 1:30 p.m. Friday."

I feel badly, and I don't know who to talk to. (At this point, the Outsidah would have pointed out, it's "whom," not "who." But it was a note, not a phone call, so I couldn't talk back.) I did start the whole vandalism spree in Ipswich on Thursday evening (the note continued), and yes, I confess, I wasn't able to finish up until — as the Ipswich Police Department reported to the *Chronicle*, making me feel like a TOTAL FOOL — after 1:30 p.m. on Friday (my bad); the reason was, and I want to make this clear, I got a text from my stepsister in Haverhill and I was just, like, Please, could you bother me at some more opportune time? I'm doing vandalism here. In Ipswich! It has to be thought through, you know what I mean? You can't just do random violence in an almost-377-year-old town! It's indecent!

I know I was stupid. The *Chronicle* exposed me. 3:19 a.m. to 1:30 p.m. They had to tell the world. (I'm like, What? Can't you keep anything secret? Have you no decency?) Yes, I know. I can do the math. I'm not so strung out on meth that I can't tell you: That's 9 hours and 11 minutes. To mess up nine vehicles and 13 mailboxes, plus the big window at Family Dollar. That's an average of 24 minutes per crime. Not very good time. It just didn't go as fast as I expected. Some places, I looked at the mailbox and I was like, Aw, that's a nice-looking mailbox, let me find a different one, and then sometimes I just couldn't decide. Plus, a lot of those car windows are made of that almost-never-breaks kind of glass. I was using my crowbar, from my historic Gloucester Man-of-the-Sea Masculinity Kit, with authentic tools from the era when we sent our men out onto the ocean to harpoon whales and hook barrels of rum from abandoned slave ships, and even my crowbar would bounce off the windshield of a 2012 Honda Accord like a paddleball. One time I accidentally konked myself in the forehead.

Anyway, I feel badly about it now. I know I inconvenienced a lot of people in Ipswich. I have a friend who had a friend who used to stay with one of their friends in an apartment above the May Flower on Depot Square when he got kicked out by his parents, and my friend was like, This is a nice town, it's a historic town, and they do good things, so if you're going to go vandalizing, and breaking windows, do it somewhere else. He was like, vandalize Danvers. Vandalize Peabody. But don't vandalize Ipswich. I have people there.

But I was like, Sorry, I was just coming up from Essex on 133 and got to the Ipswich line there at Down River Ice Cream and the speed limit goes down for no reason at all and something just came over me, and I was like, I'm gonna do me some vandalizing in this lower-speed-limit town. Smash up some lower-speed-limit cars.

Then it got complicated: The glass wouldn't break, I switched to mailboxes, I wasn't really prepared to do mailboxes, it was just hard. I didn't go to school for any of this, you know.

I was thinking next time I might try spray-paint, except I have absolutely no artistic talent. Egg-throwing? Public urination? I'm undecided. I want to make my mark, you know, but I guess I still haven't really found what I'm best at.

A TOWNIE BY ANY OTHER NAME

I am so confused.

Please help me understand the terms.

I know I'm not a "townie," but I'm not sure why I'm not.

Some folks here in Ipswich have told me that you have to have been born in Ipswich to be a townie. Which means you were born at Cable Hospital, before they closed it, or you were born in a house with an Ipswich address, perhaps with a midwife in a bonnet calmly assisting, sending your father-to-be out to heat water just to get him out of the way. To these purists, even if your family lived in Ipswich at the time of your birth, if you breathed your first air at Beverly Hospital, you're not a townie. What you are instead, I don't know. An infidel?

Then other people here in Ipswich tell me I'm not a townie because I live on Planet Outer Linebrook, beyond the gravitational pull of Marini Farm, across the Great Barrier Reef of Route 1. They use the term "townies" to refer to people who live "in town," although I'm not quite sure where "in town" ends and "out of town" starts. If you drive from my house toward Five Corners, are you "in" when you get to Our Lady of Hope? Or is Our Lady still "out"? (Could you look Pope Francis in the eye and say Our Lady isn't "in"?) Certainly if you keep driving east, and you survive Lord's Square, then you *must* be in town, right?

But then if you keep going, maybe once you get past Gordon Florist, you're "out of town" again. Or maybe you have to get past Corliss Brothers Nursery? Gordon is in but Corliss is out? I don't know. See? I'm confused.

My friend Chris Doktor lives on Town Hill, and walks to work, just over the Choate Bridge. He doesn't talk about "in town" or "out of town." He talks about "the village." This winter, when the snowbanks were higher than the gas prices, while my neighbor out here on the West Side of Nowhere was digging a tunnel to borrow a cup of sugar, you could almost see Doktor's eyes twinkling impishly over the phone: "You should live in the village," he chuckled.

Maybe there needs to be a map, with the borders clearly defined. People inside the central area would be "villagers." People outside the village but not "out of town" could be townies. (All villagers are townies, but not all townies are villagers.) People living outside the "in town" border, but inside the border with Rowley or Topsfield or Essex or Hamilton, can be "locals."

The specific borders can be negotiated by an ad hoc committee, members to be appointed by the Town Moderator, subject to confirmation by me. The specific designations assigned to residents in each of these areas can also be negotiated. Let's just agree in advance on what we will *not* call residents who live beyond Route 1.

- We don't prefer to be called "immigrants," "pioneers," or "losers." There is nothing inherently wrong with being an immigrant or a pioneer, but when residents of your own hometown use these terms, they take on a different hue.
- Kindly steer clear of "savages," "cave dwellers," and "Neanderthals."
- Also please avoid "carpetbaggers," "interlopers," and "those people."
- While we're at it, please steer clear of referring to

outer Linebrook as "P.B." for "Practically Boxford," or "East Andover."

- We are okay with "West Ipswich Farms" but don't prefer "Hillbilly Heaven," "The Ipswich Gulag," or "The Extremities."

As for calling which people what — townies, locals, natives, aborigines, whatever — I welcome your wisdom, and hope to hear from you soon. Before planting season, when I'll be with the hands, out in the fields.

PALS IN THE PIPES

I'm losing friends.

It happens every year, about this time.

The weather warms, the furnace settles in for a long summer nap, and the creatures depart. Whatever kind of creatures they are. I mean the ones that live in our radiators.

I can only assume there are creatures in there, from the sounds they make. From what I can tell, they arrive noisily in the autumn, and depart with more noise in the spring.

Of course, I would be the last one to lecture anyone on the intricacies of radiator life. Having moved to New England relatively recently, I have very little experience with these strange contraptions. To me, it seems a big cast-iron robot was squashed flat and left to die, then someone extracted its rib cage, propped it up against a wall, hooked a bent pipe into one end of it, and called it a radiator.

There was no such thing as a radiator where I grew up, outside Chicago. Our house had little rectangular vents on the walls, at floor level, where I huddled in my jammies and waited for the *whoof* of the faraway furnace and the soft, steady exhale of warm air. It was miserable when eventually, inevitably, I heard the *whup* of the furnace, as it finally inhaled in order to stay alive, and its warm breath evaporated into the morning chill.

My adult decades in Phoenix knew no radiators either. In the desert, you had a massive white box on your roof, or on a concrete pad next to your house out back, whose great challenge was to produce cold air, not hot, and enough of it to keep you alive during the nine months of summer. In the house, the vents were high on the wall, so the cool air could float down from above, dissolving into the desert atmosphere at about $4 a minute. On those five or six rare nights of the year when you needed some measure of heat, the system would grudgingly blow through the same way-up-there vents, and the warm air would hover timidly near the ceiling, wondering what it had been brought here to do.

Then we came to Ipswich, and to a 196-year-old house, already occupied by a family of 10 radiators. Most of the winter, the basement boiler rumbles, vibrating the living room floorboards, and the radiators generally sit silent, listening respectfully to the grumpy boiler below, as they glow their warmth into the air. Most of the summer, the boiler hibernates, and the radiators are empty. Abandoned. Quiet.

But in the spring and the fall, with our fickle weather and rollercoaster temperatures, the boiler gets a workout. Just when it seems he won't be needed again, a New England cold snap jerks him to life. Growling at the interruption, he begins his grumbly functions, knowing full well that it's another false alarm, and soon he will be waved off yet again: *Never mind, warm enough now.*

Meanwhile, the creatures in the radiators offer commentary. One raps a spoon against the cast iron's interior — *Pang! Pang! Pang!* — then falls silent to see if anyone raps back. Another uses a wooden stick: *Tok tok tok tok tok.* One hisses contempt: *Sssssssssss!* Another seems to have experience in the percussion section of an Asian orchestra: *Chong! Ticka-ticka-ticka. Chong! Ticka-ticka-ticka.*

From the radiator in my office, I hear the perfect imitation of an infant who has just learned to whine in a continuous sound-stream almost too high to be detected by human ears: *Eeeeeeeeee!*

In the radiator near the mudroom door, something gives the cast iron a good swift kick — *Whonk* — then seems to pat it guiltily, with a soft touch: *Pam pam pam pam pam pam.* Soon, apparently, there's another annoyance, because there's another *Whonk* — followed by more guilt: *Pam pam pam pam pam.* It's a tortured relationship, which doesn't seem to resolve until July.

Meanwhile, in the master bedroom, the radiator-creature sulks, without a sound. But I know what it's thinking: *It's broken, stupid. Call the plumber.*

No need. Soon, all the rooms will be as quiet as this one. The creatures will slip away, down through the pipes, to wherever they go.

Farewell, friends. Hello, summer.

LEARNING TO DRAW *Town Moderator Tom...*

As you read this, I'm in Minsk. It's

the capital of Belarus, a former Soviet republic. Don't
know where Belarus is? I can explain. If you find yourself
trapped between Russia, Ukraine, Poland, Lithuania, and
Latvia, you're in Belarus.

With my wife Kristina, I lead a Christian humanitarian
charity here called New Thing. (A few weeks ago,
Business Insider designated Belarus as the fourth-poorest
nation on earth, behind three African countries.)

The Western press often gripes that the KGB still
operates in Belarus. They call Belarus' president the "last
dictator in Europe." How do they know? Maybe he's only
second-to-last.

We never get into politics here. I also try to avoid
politics when I'm back home in Ipswich. But avoidance is
way easier in Minsk than in Ipswich. Here, they don't
have the "freedom of assembly" that Americans take for
granted. You need a government permit to assemble just
about any group. In Ipswich, it's the other way around.
We have Town Meeting, and you better be there, or
have a darn good excuse for why you're not.

There is no explaining Town Meeting to a Belarusian.

"The whole town comes together in one place, on a
weekday evening."

"It is revolution?"

"No, it's government."

"It is KGB?"

"No. It's everybody."

"Everybody with proper papers?"

"No, we don't do that 'Show me your papers' thing."

"How does you know who can be and who cannot?"

"Everybody is welcome. For the most part. Last year we kicked out a lawyer."

"You come to listen to president speak?"

"Ipswich doesn't have a president. We have David Wallace, who calls himself the mayor. But he's not elected. He just *is*."

"Da. We know this feeling."

"Actually, in America, we have free speech. At Town Meeting, everyone is allowed to speak."

"How does you hear anything?"

"We speak one at a time. We have a Town Moderator. He calls on each person who wants to comment, according to topic."

"He wears uniform with medals?"

"Actually, no. Usually a blazer, with a Rotary pin. But he's quite tall. People generally obey him."

"What is this word, 'topic'?"

"Ah, forgive me. I keep forgetting that English is confusingly simple. You would say предмет обсуждения. Predmet obsuzhdeniya."

"What topics are your? Nuclear bombs, I think. Terrorists. Syria."

"Those are good, yeah. But no. At Town Meeting we're more about, uh, chickens. Clams, maybe."

"Da. World hunger."

"Uh, no, actually, we're more focused on the rules. The rules about chickens. The rules about clams. We need to have permits for stuff."

"Da. We know this feeling."

"And money. Lots of discussion about money."

"How is topics deciding? Town Moderator and KGB announce new rule?"

"No, actually we all express ourselves by holding up

colored cards over our heads."

"It is game? It is American 'fun,' as you say?"

"No, the colored cards are ballots. We're voting. And whichever opinion snags the most votes, this decides the new rule."

The Belarusian falls silent. He grinds out the butt of his cigarette. He shakes his head grimly.

"It is exhausting."

Please note: Cars cannot fly.

Car commercials tell you this when they show you cars flying. There's tiny type at the bottom of the screen, warning you not to try flying your car, because cars can't fly. *Disclaimerum ad nauseum.*

Telling you "Cars can't fly" is not about "stating the obvious" taken to an extreme. It is about "reducing legal liability." Because if they show you a car flying, and you try to fly your car, and you crash, you might blame them for suggesting that cars can fly. Take them to court. Sue them for millions.

So disclaimers are important. Perhaps we need more of them.

When someone moves to Ipswich from elsewhere, as I did, some disclaimers might be helpful, in order to distinguish between what (on the one hand) seems amazing and unbelievable, and what (on the other hand) townies take for granted. Or simply to distinguish between what appears to be and what actually is. For example:

No, Selectman Pat McNally does not have a lifetime appointment.

No, the High Street bridge is not quite totally, absolutely finished yet.

Yes, you'll need a permit to change that 100-year-old electrical outlet in your parlor from a two-prong to a three-prong.

No, the building with the huge black letters that spell out "District Court" is not the District Court. Ipswich District Court is in Newburyport. Our "District Court" building is normally referred to as "Old Town Hall." No, there are no governmental activities occurring inside "Old Town Hall," unless you count the Town's lawsuit against the owner.

Yes, Town Manager Robin Crosbie actually has all those facts and figures in her head; she is not making stuff up at Board of Selectmen and FinCom meetings. When you comment on the Town's $650,000 Stabilization Fund, she will blithely lean into her microphone and — without so much as a glance at her iPad — casually advise you that it's actually $621,042.76. And she will be right. She will also whip out the maximum balance indicated in Chapter 40, Section 5-B; the amount of money sitting in the OPEB trust; the FEMA storm-related cost threshold target; which day of the week John Winthrop Jr. first landed in Ipswich; the odds of a chimpanzee learning to juggle; and how to make the tastiest possible gluten-free Boston cream pie. She is awesome. She does not actually wear a Wonder Woman costume, but she is still awesome.

No, the High Street bridge is still not quite finished. It will still need curbs, sidewalk approaches, paving, striping, according to the Massachusetts Department of Transportation Highway Division, Bridge Office, Construction Section.

Yes, to add that doorknob, you will need a permit.

Yes, the Ipswich Museum is indeed in Ipswich. You just can't find a sign pointing you to it. Good luck.

Yes, Appleton Farms does indeed straddle the line between Ipswich and Hamilton. No, milk from cows that graze on the Hamilton side does not taste like money smells. It's perfectly good milk.

Yes, it was illegal to open that window without a permit.

No, the Witches of Eastwick do not actually live here. Like many former Ipswich residents, they now live in Florida.

Yes, we have superb pothole-filling teams, and they are indeed on the job. If you encounter a pothole in our town (or an entire sinkhole, on Hayward Street), it's only because the earth under Ipswich frequently opens up and consumes asphalt. This is the same geological phenomenon that makes our terrain so perfect for clams. Those little bubbles you see in the sand at Crane Beach are the ecological equivalent of tiny potholes. If we humans lived in shells underground and breathed through tubular siphons stretching up to the surface, we would be grateful for the pockmarks of Linebrook Road and Central Street.

The High Street bridge? Look, it was officially 96% complete on February 27, according to the MassDOT website. "All substructure elements are complete." I think this means you can drive on it. You can walk on it. It will not fall down. But no. Sorry. It's not quite finished. Summer, maybe!

No, you do not need a permit to sit in the sunshine on your front step. It will, however, be voted on at Town Meeting.

The Ipswich Fire Department

recently accepted delivery on their new fire truck: a 2013 Predator Panther KME pumper. This is great because our other fire trucks are 16 and 22 years old — which is really, really old for a fire truck. Fire truck years are like dog years. Not only does a Dalmatian traditionally ride along, but the Dalmatian and the fire truck are traditionally the same age. Not really. I just made this up. But it's a very good idea. Anyway, in Ipswich's case, according to the OnlineConversion.com "Dog Years Calculator," our fire trucks are 77 and 101.

The news report about the delivery of the new fire truck included one detail that gave me pause:

"The cab features custom designed compartments to meet the demands of the Ipswich Fire Department."

What custom-designed compartments could our

Ipswich firefighters require?

I revere these guys, and I think they should have absolutely everything they could possibly want in the cab of their fire truck. So I'm hoping their wish list was really, really good.

Cup holder?

Donut holder.

Tupperware (sandwich size).

Condiment dispensing station, with pumps.

Salt & pepper shakers.

Built-in fried clam basket (clams not included).

Microwave.

Cuisinart.

Playing card dispenser.

Hands-free iPhone charging station.

Salad bar.

Oil & vinegar.

Toothpick dispenser.

Baby-changing station.

Sani-Wipes.

Magazine rack.

Mini-bar.

Washer-dryer.

X-Box dock.

Helium tank (with balloon stem).

Maybe you'll have other ideas?

Meanwhile, as reported recently by Kristina Lindborg in these pages, the Town of Ipswich has also received a used police boat — for free. It's a 25-foot Defender Class vessel, an elite law enforcement and rescue boat, which came to us as "surplus" from the U.S. Coast Guard. Buy one new, and you spend more than a quarter-million dollars. This one is only six years old — a strapping 37, in dog years. Ipswich Police Chief Paul Nikas says this type of boat is built to last 20 years — which would make it 93, in dog years, before it whimpers its last.

Ipswich got the boat thanks to patient, persistent work by the Police Department, putting in more than 30 bids for surplus boats. The feds and various state agencies repeatedly spurned us — including those creeps at the National Park Service, those creeps at the National Oceanic and Atmospheric Administration, and those creeps at the U.S. Department of Agriculture. But finally, we won one — beating out a municipality in Florida. Hooray!

I'm thinking our awesome aquatic cops should have special custom-designed compartments just like our intrepid firefighters.

Cup holder?

Donut holder.

Tupperware (sandwich size).

Condiment dispensing station, with pumps.

And so on.

Plus, maybe a cool fireworks-launcher.

If you have other suggestions, let me know. Email SafetyGuys@DougBrendel.com.

Welcome to our town!

Attend Town Meeting ... speak up ... and here you are!

CEMETERY, PARK, OR [OTHER]?

I live next door to a cemetery, which

means I can tell people, "My next-door neighbors are quiet. Because they're dead."

(Actually, this is my wife's joke, but she doesn't write a column for the *Ipswich Chronicle*, and I hate to see a perfectly good joke go to waste.)

I have not lived here long, and I was a bit, shall we say, disconcerted to learn, sometime after my arrival in town, that Ipswich has a Cemetery and Parks Department. It makes sense to me to have a Cemeteries Department. We are not barbarians; we bury our dead. People must look after our cemeteries. Especially since we have more than 375 years' worth of dead people. And it makes sense to me to have a Parks Department. Children must play, and lovers must stroll, and senior citizens must sit on benches and feed birds and read books. Also, real estate values must be maintained, and it's good for real estate values if we have pleasant places for children and lovers and senior citizens to do their aforementioned things.

But to have the "Cemeteries" and the "Parks" in the same "Department" gives me an odd feeling. It seems a bit too much melding of the living and the dead. I'm even more uneasy about having the "Cemeteries" first, before the "Parks." It's like Ipswich is hurrying me along. *Play in the park, sure — but keep moving: The cemetery is already waiting for you.*

Then one day, not too long ago, my friend David Wallace posted the following question on an Ipswich-related Facebook page:

"A Cemetery and Parks employee mowing the grass in front of the Old Town Hall today: Does anyone else find that a bit strange?"

Well, yes. I find it a bit strange.

First of all, this is the building that bears the DISTRICT COURT sign, which we locals all understand to be *not* the District Court building, but rather the "Old Town Hall." There once was a District Court inside this building, but it is no more. (A moment of silence for the dear departed.) Before it was a court, the building did indeed function as the Ipswich Town Hall. But then our government moved to a former insane asylum, which later became our high school, before becoming Town Hall. A logical progression, perhaps. (Anyway, another moment of silence for the dear departed.) And before Old Town Hall first became Town Hall, it was the Unitarian Church. (Which only lasted 10 years, then withered and went away. I guess we should offer another moment of silence for the dear departed.)

Still, in its most recent permutation, the not-a-church, not-a-court, not-Town-Hall was at least the property of the Town of Ipswich. Until we sold it to a theatre impresario, who hoped to make it a part-retail, part-jazz-club, part-performing-arts-center. But this dream died. (Another moment of, etc.) Today, the enormous, venerable edifice is tied up in court, like an aged Rolls-Royce that neither party is willing to give up in an embarrassing divorce case. It won't run, nobody can drive it, and it's rusting to death while the lawyers grunt through their slow-motion arm-wrestling match.

So a Cemetery and Parks guy mowed the grass out front. Strange, indeed. Old Town Hall is alive — architecturally valuable and potentially beautiful — but it's not quite a park. Old Town Hall is also dead — tragically neglected, decaying day by day — but it's not quite a cemetery.

Perhaps the only thing to do, in this sad limbo, is to mow the grass. Like we do for our parks. Like we do for our cemeteries. Mowing doesn't cost us much. Make it look nice. Put a proper face on it. Hope for something to happen.

I try to be reasonable. Level-

headed. Rational. I don't want to let the unimportant become important. I attempt to see the world logically. Realistically. There are too many crazies already, too many screamers and fanatics and apocalypticists.

But I fail. I am what I am. And deep inside myself, in my sub-conscious realm, in my dream-making place, I am not reasonable. Not level-headed. In fact, utterly irrational.

So this morning when I burst from my pillow in a panic, gasping and shuddering, veins throbbing in my temples, I was embarrassed to confront, yet again, my shameful personal reality.

I am tragically fixated.

Fixated on what? you may ask.

Potholes.

I was having a nightmare about the paving of outer Linebrook Road.

This is what my life has become. I'm so happy here in Ipswich, so comfortable in this town I chose, that the most serious overnight work my brain has to do is to ponder the problem of potholes.

The announcement was made — Linebrook Road would be closed from Leslie to Route 1 starting at 7 a.m. Two days for prep, two days for paving. Then, driving toward town, I saw the satisfying evidence, parked on the triangle of brush where Leslie Road doesn't know which way to turn onto Linebrook Road: a fabulous yellow Busby Construction Co. CS-563 CAT asphalt roller, its massive coffee-can wheel bulging out from its front, ready to squish hot asphalt into even the tiniest crevice.

It was love at first sight, me and this mammoth machine. Here was our great gladiator, the hero bringing healing. No more potholes spraining our spines, spilling our Starbucks, and making us miss erroneous auto-corrects while illegally texting at the wheel. Thanks to this handsome contraption, my vertebrae and my Honda's front end both have hope of realigning. Life on Planet Outer Linebrook, already very good, was about to get even better.

But in my nightmare, just as the long-awaited driver mounted the wondrous golden monster-truck, an angry crowd surged forth: residents of Mile Lane, armed with torches and clam forks. The mob engulfed the asphalt roller, climbed up into the cab, and shrieked for the driver to head east. They would have the potholes of Mile Lane filled first, or he would find himself flattened by his own device.

At this moment, I came screaming down Linebrook Road in my pajamas.

"No! No! Don't leave us! We were so close! So——"

Suddenly I fell into a pothole.

Summoning superhuman strength (this being a dream), I scrambled back up to the pocked surface of Linebrook Road. The surly horde was practically smothering the driver. Terrified, he was firing up the asphalt roller. The colossal wheels began to roll, and the pack of Mile Lane marauders sent up an awful cheer.

"No!" I screamed again.

But then — something new.

The asphalt roller abruptly stopped.

The crowd turned as one.

A straggling line of humanity had formed, most of them my Facebook friends, all the way to Route 1: dozens of citizens, from other parts of Ipswich, waving more torches and clam forks, yes, but also some angrily brandishing lacrosse sticks or backyard pub table parasols.

"Paradise Road!" Melissa Herrick hissed.

"Goldfinch Way!" Sonia Johnson growled.

Sarah MacDowell cried out over the crowd. "Dornell Road has side-by-side potholes in front of a basketball hoop! The kids will probably get swallowed up if they go out to play!"

"Hayward Street!" Judi Watts and Elizabeth McClain shouted simultaneously.

"The industrial park on Hayward will have all potholes filled very soon!" Melissa Lane chirped. "They're marked and just waiting on the company to arrive!" The crowd turned and scowled her into silence.

"Elm Street!" Sean O'Brien shouted over them. "Yes,

in front of the police station," Keith Anderson added.

"School Street, hands down!" Martha Miller yelled. Cindy Parker nodded. "Every year," Ali McClellan groused, "it buckles up."

"High Street is no picnic," Jim Martel snarled, "from Mineral to County!"

"No," Heidi Graffum-Curran jeered, "High is worse from the new bridge to ClamBox!"

"Amen!" Nancy Manning chanted. "ClamBox," Kim Marchand sneered.

"High Street toward Lord's Square," Joanna Cooper offered.

"High Street is a mess," John McGrath muttered.

"Jeffrey's Neck is a mess," Tom Palance corrected.

"Jeffrey's Neck!" Wendy Dabcovich crowed. "Takes the cake!" Kathleen Whitfield agreed.

"The Neck has some nasty ones!" Cory Simonds called out. "Especially in the rain. Under every puddle lies a hungry hole."

"Jeffrey's Neck," Jeffrey Johnson moaned, as if for a part of his own body.

"More of a sinkhole than a pothole," Barbara Parker protested.

"And Little Neck Road!" Joyce McCarthy continued.

"Did I mention," Susan McCarron mentioned, "that I broke my foot stepping into a pothole on Ryan Avenue?"

A momentary hush fell over the crowd, as David Wallace rose glowering from the mists. Solemnly he intoned:

"There's been one since winter in front of Rite-Aid,
So vast it could swallow an Ipswich parade."

"Avery Street!" Richard Hilaire barked, breaking the spell. "Quite a creative and beautiful patchwork. My grandma would be proud."

"Avery *and* Hayward!" Judi Watts declared.

"Chattanooga Road will rattle anything apart!" Daniel Rowland insisted.

"Broadway!" Denise Mootafian sang out. "And the Doyon driveway is a car-eating monster!"

"Do school parking lots count?" Nikki Weisberg asked.

"The Doyon parking lot," Lisa-Marie Cashman echoed crossly. "I've had my car realigned several times after bottoming out."

"Upper Broadway beats all," Joni Soffron said. "Hang onto your seat!" Laura Dietz seconded the m-m-m-m-motion.

"Linden Street?" Chuck Kollars crooned. "Used to be one of the town's craziest."

The crowd was growing restless, gradually advancing on the Mile Lane mob.

"Farley and Broadway," Gail Griffin groaned.

"Spillers," Allison Duback suggested.

"Jeffrey's Neck!" Wendy yelled again.

Laura Hoffmann, so far toward the back of the line she was still at work in the Library, exclaimed from the check-out desk: "Drive down Pineswamp Road to the end! There are huge orange barrels in the road warning you of the sinkholes! Not kidding!"

"The end of Pineswamp Road," Kristine Glennon prophesied, "is going to cave into the swamp!"

"The road is caving in!" Amy Bonaiuto squawked.

"Bailey," Kristen Breen asserted, "between Brownville and Perley Ave. So many people use it as a cut-through — but the town won't fix it because it isn't a 'real' road. Hang on to your coffee, and make sure everything is secured!"

"Bailey," Jason Dorr repeated.

"Bailey is a total mess," Nancy Thistlewood asserted.

The crowd settled uneasily, as David Wallace rose again from the shadows. His voice floated over the multitudes.

"At Ipswich geography, I am a whiz,
But honestly, who can say where Bailey is?"

"Never heard of it," Penny Bernard grunted.

"One block between Perley and Brownville," KelleyJane Kloub snorted.

"North Perley," Douglas Wilkins interjected.

"Town Farm," Liza Barlow whispered. "Potholes so big, you can drop an elephant into them!" KelleyJane grumped.

"I busted a strut this morning," Rose Coulombe raged, "on Town Farm Road!"

"The potholes are everywhere!" Micki Hughes yelped. "If a vehicle is coming from the opposite direction, you have to stop or risk falling into the hole. There's no way to straddle them!"

"Just confirmed," Rose grumbled: "my strut is blown. It's leaking now."

"Jeffrey's Neck!" (It was Wendy again.)

"Yeah," Kathryn Eaton sighed.

"Jeffrey's Neck now has a natural launching ramp," Heather Ann sniffed, "just before you hit the causeway. Hit it at the speed limit and you get air."

"Boxford Road, a.k.a. *far* outer Linebrook," Darcy Moulton observed.

"Central Street," Sharon West stated flatly.

"Poplar!" Julie Tucker cried out. "Heartbreak!"

Heartbreak, indeed. The crowd converged on the

hijackers, the din was deafening, the mayhem was maddening, the big yellow asphalt roller was being destroyed, carnage everywhere, twisted pieces of yellow metal flying hither and yon, each gargantuan fragment landing with a *twang* and gouging a fresh jagged pothole in Linebrook Road.

Then I woke up. Slimy with sweat, my chest heaving with the horror of it all. It was almost as if my mommy were once again sitting beside my little bed, patting my little head, in the waning days of the Eisenhower Administration, softly assuring me: "It's OK, Dougie, it was only a nightmare." At the time, she might have been referring to the Eisenhower Administration. But now, the fog began to lift. Reality began to re-emerge. Mile Lane would wait. The other streets would wait. Yes, Linebrook Road was being prepped. It would be paved. My thoracic vertebrae might eventually have a chance of disengaging from my lumbar vertebrae.

Life is good. And getting smoother.

I adapted this column from my friends' actual Facebook posts. Thanks to all who commented!

Heatherside Lane resident Jean

Barry, a faithful reader of "The Outsidah," went ballistic last week and had to sound off.

She sent me an email so hot, little puffs of exhaust squirted out of my inbox. She employed alarming phrases like "pet peeve," "drilled into your head," and "I might add," and utilized no small number of CAPITAL LETTERS.

I was relieved to realize, however, that I was not the target of Jean's rage.

She had apparently just encountered one too many pedestrians walking on the right side of the street.

Which makes her crazy.

For the sake of Jean's mental health, and for the safety of the pedestrian public, I now pass along Jean's wisdom:

When it comes to pedestrianism, *right is wrong*.

If you're walking down Linebrook Road, for example (perhaps searching for a sidewalk), it is unsafe to walk on the right side, because vehicular traffic is rushing toward you from behind, and you can't see it coming. You have no warning that a wild-eyed washing machine repairman, crazed with endorphins at the sheer thrill of escaping Saugus for the day, is about to nick you with the handlebar of his Schwinn. You can't leap into the brambles to avoid being whacked by the side-view mirror of a teenage texter in a Toyota. If your hearing is as bad as mine, you could actually be flattened by the slow-motion Marini tractor without ever realizing it.

So if you're walking on the road, you should be walking on the left. This has not only the advantage of safety — you can see the enemy approaching — but also the advantage of enhanced communication. You can offer helpful suggestions to oncoming drivers, like, "Slow down!" And your communications need not be verbal. You can, as I have often done on my own street, simply hold up a number of your fingers to indicate the speed limit which the oncoming driver is blatantly exceeding. Of course, this isn't a foolproof method. You may be holding up two fingers on one hand and five fingers on the other, indicating that the speed limit being utterly ignored is 25 mph. But if the driver is doing 40, as virtually all Ipswich drivers do, he or she will have less than two seconds to count your fingers. This may not be enough time for them to do the math.

(Let me also suggest that you resist the urge to attempt further finger-signal communications after the driver has passed you. An expression of contempt observed in one's rear-view mirror can be distracting, and cause even more danger on our roads.)

Certainly if you're the someone on the Schwinn, then the right-left rule is reversed. You shouldn't be riding your bike on the left side of the road. You're a moving vehicle, so you're supposed to be in the flow of traffic. If you ride your bike on the left side of the road, you might overrun, from behind, a good-citizen pedestrian who is properly walking on the left. This would be a tragic irony.

A number of these concerns will be beautifully addressed by the newly approved $3 million plan for repaving and redesigning Linebrook Road to make walking and biking safer. The plan was OK'd by a vote of 662 to 585 at our usual polling place, the Y. The margin might have been greater, but an unknown number of voters walking to the Y were sideswiped and sent into the weeds near Washington Street.

See? Jean's right. They should have been walking on the left.

YOU CAN'T GET THERE FROM HERE

If you are uneasy about reading

things related to "going to the bathroom," please, stop reading now. This is about "going to the bathroom."

I don't mean this biologically. I'm not talking about bodily functions. I'm just talking about walking. Starting out at the edge of your bed, which is where you're sitting when you realize you need to go to the bathroom, and then walking, from your bed, to your bathroom.

It should be a simple matter. But this is New England.

New England is the land of blocked-off doorways. In our antique houses, with our nooks and crannies and rooms added on 180 years after the house was built, we wind up with doors where we don't need them. Yet there's a certain Yankee reluctance to spend the time, energy, and money it would take to make it just a plain wall, when there's a chance that in 60 or 70 years, you'll want a doorway there again. So it's not uncommon to see a couch in front of a door, or a chair or a lamp or a table in front of a door — and the owners don't even think of it as a door anymore. It's just a wall that seems to look like a door. Yes, it was a doorway, with people actually walking through it, from James Knox Polk to Millard Fillmore, and again from Grover Cleveland to Warren G. Harding. But the whole rest of the time, basically it's just been a wall.

There's one room in our house where this becomes really serious business. After 200 years of nook-adding and cranny-shifting and space-narrowing and corridor-widening, our house has ended up with one tiny room which has not a single window, but four doors. From this little roomlet, you can get to the guest room, the laundry room, the living room, or a bent little passageway too small to be called a hall. The room is all doors. There is only one precious wall where you can put a piece of furniture without worrying about who will be entering, exiting, bumping, slamming, or otherwise ricocheting through.

What to do with such an odd little place? We are not big TV watchers, so we stuck our TV in here. There's really no other use for this space. Well, this isn't quite true. I have indeed used this odd little room for something else. A single, simple function.

I walk through it on my way to the bathroom.

I abandoned the upstairs bathroom because — I trust it's not too sexist to say — it was overrun by females. As the only guy in the household, I took ownership of the downstairs bathroom. Getting there and back was no problem at all. Until I went out of town for a couple weeks, and my wife decided to rearrange the furniture in the odd little TV room.

So now, instead of slipping downstairs and heading straight to the bathroom, with only one little sidestep along the way — well, that sidestep is now a closed door with a brown couch standing guard in front of it.

Which means, from my bed, I cross the room diagonally, out the bedroom door, hang a right on the landing, down three stairsteps, left, seven more steps, another left, last three stairs, then a right, diagonally across the living room, into the kitchen, wide arc around the table and chairs, into the bent little passageway too small to be called a hall, sharp left, one step into the accursed TV room (making a certain gesture toward the brown couch), hang a left into the laundry room hallway, and a sharp right into the bathroom.

I am planning today to go to the bathroom on Tuesday. Packing a light lunch for the trip.

◀ Jun 2013

Aug 2013

~ July 2013 ~ ▶

Sun	Mon	Tue	Wed	Thu	Fri	Sat
	1 Curse the rain	2 Curse the rain	3 Curse the rain	4 Mow the grass	5 Curse the rain	6 Mow the grass
7 Curse the rain	8 Curse the rain	9 Mow the grass	10 Curse the rain	11 Curse the rain	12 Mow the grass	13 Mow the grass
14 Curse the rain	15 Curse the rain	16 Mow the grass	17 Curse the rain	18 Mow the grass	19 Curse the rain	20 Curse the rain
21 Mow the grass	22 Curse the rain	23 Curse the rain	24 Curse the rain	25 Curse the rain	26 Mow the grass	27 Curse the rain
28 Curse the rain	29 Mow the grass	30 Curse the rain	31 Curse the rain	Notes:		

ONLY GUNS WILL HAVE NECKS

"If you outlaw guns," they say,

"only outlaws will have guns."

So what happens if you ban Ipswichers from Little Neck? Only Ipswichers will have necks? Only Little Neckers will have guns? I'm already confused, and the column has hardly begun.

The *Chronicle* reported recently in these pages that Little Neck is now officially closed to everybody in the whole wide world except for the folks who own or rent property there. No Japanese tourist, no Kenyan exchange student, no Tibetan monk seeking to commune with the universe will be allowed to set foot on these 31 or so hallowed acres of Massachusetts rock. Little Neck has become the equivalent of a gated community. Go there without an invitation to someone's party, and the handcuffs come out.

I have no way in. I had one solitary friend on Little Neck, and he died. I loved him dearly, he went suddenly, far too young. I still feel a lump in my throat whenever I think of him, and I think of him every day. Certainly, if he had lived in Rowley, or North Reading, or West Newbury, I would have felt just as badly. But since he was a lifetime year-round resident of Little Neck, I can't help but also bear the guilty burden of this additional truth: If he had lived, he could have gotten me onto Little Neck!

Now there's no way I can get there. There are some 167 properties, none of them occupied by my "friends." At least none I can call up and casually snag an invitation to wander there on a lazy spring afternoon. Even if I make nice with our selectmen, I can't *brrrrr* in and out of there some Sunday morning hanging onto the back of Pat McNally's motorcycle. I can't paddle my damaged boat to the shore of Little Neck and trudge, humiliated, up to River Road, to plead with a local resident for help — for fear of a law enforcement officer appearing, like Columbo, scratching the back of his head: "Excuse me, sir, I couldn't help but notice your boat here, on the edge of this private property. You know, of course, there's a trespassing lawr, and you seem to have broken it heah."

Little Neck is an inside-out prison. The inmates are kept outside.

Of course, there is the Little Neck Condo

Association, the homeowners' group that controls the property now. They could hand down an edict from on high, allowing you as an Ipswich resident to meander in your Nike walking shoes on their sacred ground, maybe even ride your 26-inch Huffy "Alpine" mountain bike on their self-maintained, self-trash-picked-up, self-snow-plowed roads. They could let everyone enjoy Little Neck. They haven't, but they could.

Still, I have an idea. There are houses for sale on Little Neck. In the same issue of the *Ipswich Chronicle* in which I first read about Little Neck being closed off to most human beings, I also read that one could purchase a Middle Street property on Little Neck for as little as $565,000. This seems like a good deed waiting to happen.

Here's what I'm thinking.

Little Neck trespassers will be legion. The allure of Little Neck as a destination for walkers, runners, cyclists, and gawkers ("Look! Look there! An off-limits resident in her kitchen window!") will be irresistible. Law enforcement? A nightmare.

We will need a jail. Chief Nikas will not have enough of his pink-walled cells available for the overwhelming influx of Little Neck lawbreakers.

I will set up a non-profit organization — Little Neck, Limited, get it? — buy a property on Little Neck, and set it up as a holding pen for trespassers.

OK, maybe it won't be an actual jail. Maybe more of a halfway house. A place where the Little Neck Trespass Police drag you, reading you your rights en route, then handcuff you to a chair under a dim light bulb, extract your trespassing fine, and then — here's a nice touch, I think — start you on rehab. We'll have a social worker on staff who interviews you, subjects you to a battery of tests, assesses the results, and then attempts to rehabilitate your Little Neck addiction with one of two strategies, whichever is more appropriate for your individual state of mind:

1. "It's a dump." The social worker attempts to persuade you that Little Neck isn't worth trespassing on. She says things like "I had a nicer timeshare in Swampscott" and "Before you know it, this place will be swimming in its own sewage."

2. "Other fish in the sea." The social worker takes you on little excursions, to acclimate you to alternative Ipswich walking routes. "See here?" she says gently at the foot of the Cedar Point Trail on Steep Hill Beach. "This is a nice walk, isn't it? And you can see Little Neck from here. No, don't look away. It's healthier to face your grief. Oh, you're crying again. Come on, let's try a nice stroll on 133. I'll buy you an ice cream."

In days to come, you may strike up a conversation with a stranger in Zumi's. If they say, "Hi, my name is Doug, I'm a recovering Little Neck trespasser," please don't snicker. Just give online, and help me help more of these poor souls.

Wait, wait. My wife has a better idea. Our non-prof will buy the house on Middle Street, and simply invite everybody over as our guests. Everyone in the whole wide world! Much simpler plan.

At the guardhouse, just say, "The Brendels invited me."

However, while you're on Little Neck, please — behave well. I don't want my new neighbors to feel I'm bringing in riff-raff.

HONEST, OFFICER

I subscribed to the *Ipswich Chronicle*

months before I actually arrived in town to take
occupancy of my new/old house. I enjoyed the paper
very much, but I was truly mesmerized by the Police Log.
It seemed to reveal that my new hometown-to-be was
another kind of world. A number of entries seemed to
paint a completely unexpected picture in my imagination:

12:16 p.m. Suspicious items found were reported on
Lafayette Road.

10:35 a.m. A suspicious phone call was reported on High Street.

6:25 a.m. Suspicious "No Parking" signs on South Main Street were reported.

6:50 p.m. Someone banging on the door was suspicious on High Street. (Like banging on the door wouldn't be all that suspicious on, say, Town Farm Road?)

12:15 p.m. Malicious property damage was reported on Lafayette Road. (As opposed to the friendly property damage we used to do in Chicago.)

7:17 p.m. Simple threats were made on Kimball Avenue. ("I don't want this to be complicated, dear. If you don't shut up, I'm going to kill you.")

8:22 p.m. A simple assault was reported on Kimball Avenue. (*Whack!* "Well, that wasn't too complicated, was it?")

4:10 p.m. A dog complaint was made on North Ridge Road. Animal Control advised a resident of the leash law. (What does this mean? What happened? "Hello, police? This is Rover, I'm a beagle here on North Ridge Road, and my owner refuses to put me on my leash.")

11:11 a.m. A kayak complaint was made on Little Neck Road. (Of course a kayak is going to complain. "Hey, can't you please put me in the water?")

2:39 a.m. Officers checked on a person urinating in public on South Main Street. A summons was issued. (I'm thinking, issue a diaper!)

9:19 a.m. Police checked on people in an unoccupied apartment on Southern Heights. (If it's unoccupied, how are there people in it?)

10:10 a.m. An officer checked on a vehicle occupied by a feline on River Road. ("Meow! To you it's just a

Volvo, but to me, it's home.")

11:12 a.m. A person walking and looking confused was reported on Linebrook Road. ("No officer, I'm not really confused, I just look this way!")

Sometimes there are little action movies in the Police Log:

5:13 p.m. An officer made a motor vehicle stop for speeding on Linebrook Road at Marini's Farm.

5:24 p.m. An officer made a motor vehicle stop for speeding on Linebrook Road at Leslie Road.

5:28 p.m. An officer made a motor vehicle stop for speeding on Linebrook Road at Plains Road.

This driver just does not learn, does he!

9:01 p.m. An unwanted party was reported on Lafayette Road. (What does this mean? "Officer, I told my husband I didn't want a party this year. I hate it that I'm turning 40. But now look what he did! Balloons, and streamers!")

11:14 p.m. An unwanted guest was reported on Kimball Avenue. ("Officer, I told my husband I didn't want a party this year. But now look what he did! He invited Harold!")

I went ahead and moved here anyway. I still love the Police Log. Except now it's about my neighbors. And me!

Did you receive the notice?

"It has come to the attention of the Water Department that many customers have received a mailing from a private company recommending a water sample be sent to them for testing."

This company, the Water Department says, is not affiliated with the Town of Ipswich. They're just soliciting business for water filters.

"The Water Department would like to reassure any concerned customers that their water is safe and meets or exceeds all state and federal water quality parameters."

If the mailing doesn't work, I imagine they'll ramp up a telemarketing campaign. Soon your phone will ring.

"Mrs. Schloshmacher, I'm calling because of concerns in the Town of Ipswich about the water supply. Have you noticed a somewhat strange taste in your tap water yet?"

"Oh my."

"Now, there's no reason to be alarmed, quite yet anyway, Mrs. Schloshmacher. We can help you."

"What's wrong with my water?"

"Well, you know, water has a certain chemical makeup, and the latest samples of Ipswich water indicate that it may contain twice as much hydrogen as oxygen."

"Oh dear."

"Also, we've run studies on your Ipswich water, and in laboratory testing, it is actually not very stable."

"Really!"

"We've tested it on inclines and irregular surfaces, and we've found that it tends to move downhill. Very disturbing."

"I had no idea!"

"At certain low temperatures, we've found that Ipswich water actually gets stiff, sometimes even solid, and stops flowing at all. But we've also tested it at high temperatures and, I'm sorry to report, your Ipswich water often literally disappears. You're paying for water, and you wind up with nothing."

"That is an outrage!"

"We have found also that your Ipswich H2O dissolves certain substances."

"My, my."

"You don't want to be taking your bath in something that *dissolves* stuff, do you?"

"I don't know what to say!"

"And maybe most tragic of all, for the unsuspecting people of Ipswich, your Town water has been linked to *drownings.*"

"Horrible! What can I *do*, young man?"

"I really believe, for your own protection, you need to order our water purification system. For just $139.95, you can have complete confidence that the water you drink, and cook with, and bathe in, is as safe as can be."

"Oh, yes, this sounds wonderful. I am so grateful. Bring it as quickly as possible, *please.*"

"I think you're making a wise decision, ma'am. I'll arrange for our representative to be out there tomorrow. But since you do live in Ipswich, let me also ask you one more very important question: Have you noticed that somewhat strange smell in your *air?*"

Once in a rare while, my astute first-reader-editor-wife says, "No, that's too weird to submit to the Chronicle." I'm always offended, of course, and I quietly move the rejected column to the pile designated for "the book only." What follows is the worst of what Kristina rejected this past year.

IMAGINE, ME

When I was in Congress, things

were not as polarized as they are now. We talked to each other, we recognized that nobody could get everything they wanted, but to keep the country moving, we agreed to trade various preferences and priorities, and everything moved along more or less comfortably. Today, it's just honking for the camera and running for re-election. It's disgusting.

When I was in Paul McCartney's studio band, things were simpler. You didn't have to deal with the crowds of crazies, and the drug dogs in the airports.

The Nobel Prize really meant nothing to me. I'm serious.

There's a part of me that wants more credit for the time I put in as Elizabeth Taylor's husband. I realize that I was only one among many, but still. I felt I dealt with her idiosyncrasies graciously. R.I.P., Liz.

I know it's more challenging now for Eric Colville than it was for me when I was the assistant building inspector for the Town of Ipswich. Even so, I don't think Eric needs to cuss so much.

It makes me smile to think about how crazy we were, trying to paint a mural depicting the history of Ipswich on the side of the EBSCO building. It should have been obvious to us, from the moment we started talking about the project, that we needed someone of Alan Pearsall's talent level. I was crazy even to try. But I must say, those were two pretty fun years, all that painting and then painting over what I'd already painted.

I am very honored and humbled that anyone would ever associate me with the building of the old High Street Bridge, but this is simply a myth that somehow sprang up. I didn't design it, I didn't have anything to do with the building of it, and I didn't contribute in any way to whatever inferior aspects of its design or construction made it necessary to tear it down and totally replace it.

Quite a number of notable people have served the Town of Ipswich as selectmen at some point down through the years, and I completely understand and sympathize with those who don't have fond memories of that time in their lives. But I have to say, for myself, I found it a completely rewarding experience, and I would not trade those three years for anything.

The other day, when Prince George was born in England, I couldn't help but remember those deeply meaningful days when — between med school and working with that clamming crew in Rowley — I was privileged to wait on Princess Diana in my capacity as Royal Cobbler. So grateful I took that cobbling course, on a seeming whim, at Katmandu U.!

Life is great. I am down to two days a week in therapy, and I really feel I am getting my ego in line with reality. Also, I am making significant progress on the sleepwalking problem, according to my somnambulologist. This morning I found another surprising screen full of stuff on my computer, but I feel confident that it was not the result of another of my middle-of-the-night trances. This one seems to me the kind of thing that Doug Brendel would slip in and type as a joke. I haven't had one of those "I imagine I'm Doug Brendel" dreams in quite some time.

IPSWICH UNDERGROUND

In the relatively short time I've been

here, I feel I've learned pretty well how to get around
town. I know the difference between County Road and

County Street. In case of a late-night brush with the law, I can get to the homes of three out of five selectmen. I know the shortcut from the Masonic Lodge to Bialek Park. (Of course this is not all that valuable, since very few Masons play on the swings.)

However, I'm having a problem finding the new subway.

From the moment I heard the great news — "Ipswich is getting a subway!" — I was thrilled. I haven't yet been able to find the ticket office, or any of the stations, but I'm sure a subway is going to make this an even more livable place. I imagine the subterranean tracks extending from Crane all the way to my house on Planet Outer Linebrook, with stops at Family Dollar, Rite-Aid, the ClamBox, and Marini Farm. There might also be a stop at Little Neck where you're not allowed to get off.

Train travel totally beats driving. It's exhilarating to think that soon, I might never again need to play chicken with a vehicle that's turning left when the light turns green at Route 1, or squeal my brakes behind someone at Lord's Square who thinks you have to stop at High Street. Ipswich's overall productivity will soar as residents save a cumulative 147,282 hours a month which they now spend doing hand signals to negotiate their vehicle across Five Corners.

It's remarkable to me that they were able to put in a subway, with our water table so high. I suppose it was hardly a challenge, though, if they hired former Big Dig engineers.

I've also heard that a number of folks in Ipswich were against us getting a subway. I must say, I'm glad that the sensible view prevailed. And really, when you think about it, an Ipswich subway is the ideal way to preserve our official "open spaces." You could be on Greens Point Road, looking out across the magnificent marsh, and never know that the 3:04 is rumbling along under it all, with a payload of nuns heading to the Sisters of Notre Dame stop after a long, lazy day at the beach.

But figuring out how to actually get on the new Ipswich subway has proven to be problematic for me.

My friend John Baran, an otherwise intelligent and erudite professional who works in the education field, is as confused, and as eager, as I am. We were on adjacent stationary bicycles in the fitness room at the Y this past weekend when he told me about a puzzling conversation with another local. "Where do you work?" John asked him. "The new subway," the guy replied. "Taking tickets?" John asked. "No," the guy replied, "chopping lettuce."

"Chopping lettuce!" I exclaimed, pumping my bicycle even faster. "John! Maybe the Ipswich subway station has a Taco Bell! I love Taco Bell! We gotta find this place!"

Alas, this takes us back — as always — to the issue of the Ipswich town budget. At the last minute, the $30,000 line item for signage was cut. No new signs for Ipswich. Which means, sadly, nobody can find the new Ipswich subway.

Nor the Taco Bell.

I CANNOT RECALL

I am really sorry you missed it. I

attended last week's "Music at the Meetinghouse," part
of the wonderful new "Ipswich, Down Town Tuesdays"
series of free community events, the brainchild of Kerrie
Bates, director of the Ipswich ReCreation and Culture
Department.

Some 90 people jammed into the First Church
Meetinghouse — straining the limits of legal occupancy
for the historic structure — for a great evening of music

and poetry, with refreshments donated by local businesses. The event began with a very talented young singer-songwriter. A passionate poet then read a number of his pieces. Finally, the star of the evening took the stage.

Backed by a brilliant standing-bass player and an excellent drummer, he sang a number of his own songs, as well as a fine selection of songs written by others. He wasn't able to recall the names of any of the other writers, but that's OK. We writers are used to this.

Anyway, the featured performer was great. I could understand why he's widely regarded as a New England treasure. I actually can't remember his name at the moment, but I do remember he was born and raised in Ipswich. He has emerged as a super-talented singer-songwriter, with gigs all over the North Shore. I just can't quite recall — do you know who I mean? His boyish good looks are balanced by gently graying hair, which he wears a little long and casual. Neville, maybe? No, that's the guy who did that duet with Linda Ronstadt. This guy has a beautiful smile and a sparkling sense of humor, a warm way with an audience. I'm trying to think — the moment you say it, I'm going to kick myself for forgetting. His voice is supple and versatile — he handled a wide array of musical styles, from Nat King Cole jazz to rockabilly to soulful folk, all with ease — and he's a truly dazzling guitarist. Darn, what is that sucker's name? It's remarkable that he isn't doing music fulltime, but in real life (although I imagine most folks in Ipswich don't know this), he labors as a gardener. Maybe you could support the North Shore music scene by hiring him to trim your shrubs or something. If only I could tell you whom to contact. I think one of his names starts with a vowel.

Audie, maybe? Otto?

Now I feel badly. I didn't mean anything by my comment about his not being able to remember the names of the other writers. It's true, every time he tried to tell the audience the name of the person who wrote the song he was about to sing, he stumbled, fumbled, and turned to his band for help — and they didn't remember either. Of course, I've been a writer my entire adult life, so I might have taken offense at this, except that after a lifetime of people remembering everything about a book or a movie or a song *except* the name of the person who wrote it, I'm more or less accustomed to this universal disrespect for the creative people who drive our entire culture. It's a shrug of the shoulders for me. Honest.

So let me just say, this radiant talent — wait, I think I've got it: Orson. No. Owen. No. I'll get it. Just give me a minute.

BANISHED

That rattling in the ceiling?

That's squirrels, skittering about in the attic of my antique house, living up there without even offering to pay rent or do any of the household chores.

I wonder how they got in there, until I notice a gaping hole chewed in one corner of my roof. A ragged aperture, and growing. Where once there was a beautiful angle, the roof pleasingly connecting to the exterior wall in the style of the era — now the point of connection is ragged, an open scab on my beloved 1817 Federal

Period house. *Hee hee!* the squirrels seem to snicker. *We've bitten a hole in your history!*

What alarms me most was that they've put in a doorway without a single Town of Ipswich permit. This could mean penalties — serious fines — possibly loss of membership in the assistant building inspector's fan club. These wretched rodents could ruin my finances *and* my social life — on top of the ugly cavity they've gnawed.

How to fight back? I am helpless. My primary experience with squirrels is *tsk-tsk*ing as I drive by their squashed carcasses on Linebrook Road. ("Too bad," my heathen side mutters. Then my religious side takes over: "Give rest, Lord, to the soul of Your servant [insert squirrel's name here] who has fallen asleep, where there is no pain, sorrow, or suffering. In Your goodness and love for all, pardon all the sins he [she] has committed in thought, word, or deed, for there is no [squirrel] who lives and sins not. Amen.")

In my besieged home, I need help. My squirrel-squatters are eating my mortgaged wood; they have apparently failed to qualify for food stamps. My domicile is being decimated, nibble by nibble. I need a pest professional. A varmint vanquisher.

The uniformed professional who pulls into my driveway is nonchalant. He shrugs. He has fought this evil before, and prevailed. He is armed not with a gun or a poison, but with a small, squirrel-sized door. He climbs up a very tall ladder and affixes the door over the dreadful defect. If I didn't have trouble with the Ipswich building inspector before, I am sure to now.

But this is no ordinary door. This door only opens one way: *out*. A squirrel can leave the comfy confines of my attic, but when he tries to return....

"Honey, I'm home!"
(Skittering and scratching sounds from inside.)
"Honey, it's locked!"
(More squirrel sounds.)
"Honey, come on. Open up."
"Harold? Is that you?"
"What do you mean, 'Harold, is that you'? Do you

normally have guys coming to visit you when I'm not home?"

"Harold, why are you outside? Come in the house!"

"I'm trying to tell you, woman! I'm locked out!"

"Oh, for Pete's sake. I didn't lock the door."

"Will you please just open it?"

"It opened just fine when you left for work this morning."

"I know that! But it doesn't seem to be working now!"

(Skittering sounds. The door swings open. She steps out.)

"Look. It works perfectly. You are so squirrelly."

"Thanks a lot. I love you too."

(The door slams behind her.)

"Oh, great. Bang on the door. The kids can let us in."

"The kids went to the park."

(They stare at each other for a long moment.)

"This is how it went for Adam and Eve too, isn't it."

"I hate moving."

GREENHEADS ARE PEOPLE TOO

Two greenheads are dressing in the

women's locker room after a long day at Crane Beach.

"Good summer?"

"Nah, not that great."

"Me neither."

"Took a chunk out of Brenda McCarthy today. No big deal."

"I got Heidi Bartlett last week."

"Don Francis in Week 1. Shoulda heard him howl!"

"But such a rainy summer. One day I had to fly all the way to Mitchell Road to find an exposed neck. Got some farmer lady in an orchard."

"Just doesn't seem to be as much fun as it was when we were young."

"Yeah."

"I remember that first summer on the marsh, as a little larva. Almost 200 of us. Starving! Mucking through the mud and the thatch, hungry for anything."

"I found an earthworm that summer."

"I ate my brother."

"You do what you have to do, I guess."

"Gotta bulk up to form that pupa, so you can hunker down for that first winter."

"It is New England, after all."

"But then — wow! Busting out of that pupa in the spring — *kapow!* Hormones!"

"I know, right? I was like, Where's Mr. Right? Aw, heck, you'll do!"

(A sigh.) "It was good, that first time."

"Yeah, but then *wham!* You're pregnant! And then

wham! You're delivering. And delivering, and delivering."

"I guess it just goes with being a *Tabanus nigrovittatus*. I had 192 larvae my first time out."

"And then, the moment they wheel you into recovery, *kaboom!* The hunger pangs! Out of nowhere! You've never had a drop of blood in your life, but for some reason, all of a sudden, you can't think of anything but the red stuff."

"That summer, there was nobody, I mean *nobody*, on the beach."

"I just started going house to house. I bit Mr. Wasserman."

"Good for you."

"But this year has been the worst. So many good flies disappearing into those black boxes."

"I try to tell them, 'Don't do it! It's a trap!' But they're all like, 'It's big and dark like a horse or something, and *I'm starving!*' And zip! They're gone."

"It's sad. I lost almost a thousand of my closest girlfriends in a single hour last month."

"I swear, I've thought about just throwing in the towel. Shoot into a black box, hang up the ol' bra, call it a day."

"Ginny! No!"

"I'm tellin' ya, I've had 857 kids this summer, and I'm tired."

"You'll feel better soon. I'm sure of it. Our life cycle isn't that long."

"I'm sick of this! The men don't go out and hunt for blood. The men don't plop down in the mucky marsh and pop out 150 babies at a time. The men don't have to dodge flyswatters and bite horse skin and have their dinner punctuated by shrieking children. For the men, it's just sex and veggies, sex and veggies. Nectar! Fruit juice! They have no need for blood protein! They live on carbs! I hate them!"

"Ginny, come on. Hey. I love that green eye shadow."

"Don't try to make me feel better. You're always so cheery. 'Ipswich! We get to live in Ipswich!' Like a world-class beach somehow makes it OK that you have 857 kids."

"Well, you don't exactly have to take care of them all. I mean, look, you're not a mother duck."

"The greenhead life is a drag, Doris. It's all strategy, strategy, strategy. I got Penny Bernard by waiting under the top of her boat. I got Valda Winsloe on the river. But it's getting harder and harder. Chuck Kollars doesn't even roll down the windows of his PT Cruiser during most of July. I got all the way to Jim Engel's place on outer Linebrook, looked around, and I was the only fly around. It was embarrassing."

"I know, honey. Things will get better."

"I'm tired of being written up on Wicked Local. I'm tired of landing on a slathering of Skin So Soft and spending the next hour licking it off. *Glecch!*"

"Come on, let's go get something to drink. There's a Catholic family having a backyard barbecue this evening. A bloody Mary will do you good."

Sometimes I poll my friends on Facebook and use their responses to write "The Outsidah." Like in the case of "Greenheads Are People Too." If you're not on Facebook, contact me via Outsidah.com.

Thank heaven I don't live in Beverly.

I attend a monthly meeting on Rantoul Street, and I always forget to bring quarters for the parking meter. To find a parking space without a meter, I have to drive halfway back to Wenham, then hike to the meeting.

Thank heaven I don't live in Newburyport. In their huge downtown parking area, which used to be free, you have to park your car, get out of your car, close the car door, walk to a kiosk, pay the parking fee, collect your sticker, walk back to your car, open the door, stick the sticker on your windshield, close the door again — by which time you're too weary to shop.

Thank heaven we live in Ipswich. If you want to park downtown, to shop at any of our fine downtown stores, or eat in any of our fine downtown dineries, you have multitudinous free-parking options. The parking is free on Central Street, on South Main, on Market Street, on Depot Square, and on Hammatt Street.

But best of all, we have a sprawling rectangle of parking available on Hammatt, behind the stores on the south side of Central, behind the shops on the west side of Market. If you find yourself between Ithaki's awesome upscale dining location and the Ipswich Sports Bar's not-upscale-but-also-awesome dining location — you can point your vehicle north and within 10 seconds you will come to the Hammatt Street parking lot, on your right. There is no signage on Central or Market to indicate that you can park here, but please, take it from me, "The Outsidah" — I have checked this out.

Welcome.

We're glad you're here.

Thank you for coming to Ipswich.

We're grateful that you've decided to spend your disposable income in our town.

Parking is free! This isn't Newburyport. This isn't Salem. This isn't even Peabody. This is Ipswich. Park wherever you like.

To make your parking experience as carefree as possible, please allow "The Outsidah" to take you on a brief tour of the Hammatt Street parking lot. This will really be very simple.

1. Look for the conventional "P" sign, indicating "Parking." Our "P" is on a telephone pole, which also sports signs which say BROWN SQ and STOP. If you go to the west, you come to the Ipswich Ale brewery. If you have a designated driver, go ahead and turn to the west. Otherwise, turn east.
2. The most obvious place to turn in to the Hammatt Street parking lot is across from Lake Legal. The sign says LAKE LEGAL LLC. Turn east.
3. The first sign you come to says: "FIRST Ipswich BANK EMPLOYEE PARKING Weekdays 8 AM to 5 PM FRIENDS & CUSTOMERS PARKING Evening & Weekends." Ignore this sign. Continue driving into the parking area.
4. The next sign you come to says: "FIRST Ipswich BANK PARKING FOR BANK EMPLOYEES ONLY Violators will be Towed at the Vehicle Owners Expense M.G.L. 266S.120A,D." If you find that you are too intimidated by this sign to park your vehicle here, back out onto Hammatt Street and proceed to the next parking lot entrance.
5. The next entrance is even simpler. You will find a

warm welcome here. The sign says: "Welcome to the Hammatt Street Parking Lot A jointly owned lot with municipal parking spaces designated in BLUE for public use. Privately Owned Spaces Have Additional Signage. RULES AND REGULATIONS * Please Park in Designated Spaces * Short-term parking ONLY in Non-Designated YELLOW Coded Areas * Handicapped Spaces by Permit Only * Overnight Parking by Permit Only Permits Issued by Ipswich DPW * Abandoned Vehicles Will Be Towed CLEANING/SNOW REMOVAL Cleaning Regulations effective from April 15 through November 15. Snow Removal Regulations effective from November 15 through April 15. Regulations Available from Ipswich Police & DPW."

If you are uneasy about parking here because the signage is a little overwhelming, I understand. It was a little overwhelming to me too, until I got my degree. But a quick tour of the Hammatt Street parking area will help to ease your fears. If we simply drive the circumference of the entire parking lot, we can observe the various parking-related signs, and we can see clearly how simple it will be for us to park our vehicle freely just about anywhere we want to park it. Turning to our left, and making our way around the edge of the entire paved area, here's what we find:

6. "Parking For Super Subs" (arrow to the right). Not sure exactly where they mean, but don't park someplace close to their sign, and you'll probably be OK.

7. "TD Bank R ERVED ANK USTOMER." This sign, overgrown by foliage, is probably historical. Ignore it.

8. A series of seemingly open parking spaces are barred by yellow stamps: "PRIVATE MSP." Park here? Don't park here? Not sure.
9. Two HILTZ RECYCLING dumpsters say: "DO NOT PARK." I think this means "Do not park in front of these dumpsters."
10. A sign on the back of a building says: "TENANT PARKING ONLY VIOLATORS WILL BE TOWED AT OWNERS EXPENSE." The realty named at the bottom of the sign doesn't even show up on a Google search.
11. Next there's a dumpster that says: "JRM Hauling & Recycling DO NOT PARK."
12. Next there's a dumpster that says: "TRASH ONLY G. MELLO DISPOSAL CORP. DO NOT PARK OR BLOCK."
13. Then there are a few signs that say: "PARKING For: Tenants of 7-9 Market St. ONLY," followed by a sign it seems somebody tried to tear down, which says: "NO PARKING UNAUTHORIZED VEHICLES WILL BE (and then there's a big blank space) AT VEHICLE OWNER'S EXPENSE." *What will they do to those poor vehicles?*
14. Then there are the sadly conventional "PARKING FOR RESIDENTS & CUSTOMERS OF 15 MARKET STREET ONLY ALL OTHERS WILL BE TOWED AT THEIR OWN EXPENSE" and "15 MARKET STREET CUSTOMER PARKING ONLY NO OVERNIGHT PARKING" and "PERMIT PARKING ONLY 9:30PM through 8:30AM VIOLATORS TOWED AT OWNERS EXPENSE."
15. Then there's a good old-fashioned "NO PARKING."
16. Finally! We find a series of open parking spaces! But

— sorry — the message painted in yellow on the edge of this section of the parking lot is (I kid you not): NO PARKING.

17. Continuing our tour of the Hammatt Street parking lot brings us to a black dumpster which says DO NOT PARK.
18. Then there's a red garage door with an orange NO PARKING sign.
19. Then there's a black plastic dumpster that says, very plainly, DO NOT PARK IN FRONT OF CONTAINER.
20. Then there's a delicious space behind the Ipswich Sports Bar that's *perfect* for parking, and not a single sign telling you not to.
21. And finally, there's a beautiful, old, seemingly abandoned red brick building on Hammatt, with a great big number 18 on it, and not a single DO NOT PARK or NO PARKING or PRIVATE or any other scary sign.

See? The Hammatt Street parking lot is here for *you.* Thank heaven we live in Ipswich. Parking is free.

On the Occasion of

A birthday poem? No problem writing that.
There are a lot of words to rhyme with "Pat."
He has no hair, and so he wears a *hat*.
He's our town's longest-serving bureau*crat*.

You'll find, if you and Pat should have a *chat*,
He is a simple guy: he's no fat *cat*,
No snobbish, arrogant aristo*crat*.
And on that leg, he's quite the acro*bat*.

Now if you have an ugly legal *spat*,
No lawyer is superior to *Pat*.
You see your marriage going up in flames?
Just trust the ol' divorce whiz, Patrick James.

For open space all over our locale,
We owe a major debt to Pat McNal.
But most important, Pat's a faithful friend.
And with this truth, my po-em now will end.

Speak of the Devil

I was hunkered down on my screen

porch, surfing Facebook on my laptop as usual, when I heard a familiar voice.

"Well, hello there."

It was the sultry voice of my wife. But she wasn't talking to me. I craned my neck to find her through the screen.

"How are you?" she said.

She was in her gardening gear, standing on the narrow path between the breezeway and the backyard. Not looking at me. Not even looking up. She was looking down. Onto the path itself.

"You're not going anywhere, are you," she said, more as a statement than a question.

I had to get up and go look. At the edge of the screen, I could finally see who her boyfriend was. It was a garter snake, maybe two-and-a-half feet long. He was lying perfectly still, but with his head angled up, looking at my wife.

"Hmph," the fearless woman finally said. She nonchalantly stepped around the snake and went on her way.

It was quite some time, long after she had left to run errands, that I found myself on the same path. The snake was now stretched out completely across the walkway, from a mound of mulch on one side to the lilies of the valley on the other, blocking my way. I had no choice but to go on the offensive.

"Who do you think you are," I demanded, "ogling my wife like that?"

"It's no sss*in*, is it," the snake hissed, "to look at a pretty lady?"

"What do you know about sin?" I asked. "Are you Satan?"

"Not sss*sayin'*," he replied.

"I didn't expect snakes in Ipswich," I offered. "Before I moved here, I thought of it as an old-fashioned colonial-era village: prim, square houses lined up on cobblestone streets, with lampposts."

"*Sssilly* boy. Look around. You live on Planet Outer Linebrook. You're on the wrong end of town if you wanted prim and cobblestone and lampposts. You've got woods and meadows and Hood Pond, for cryin' out loud. This is sssnake heaven."

"How long have you lived on my property?"

"I was born the day you arrived. I've lived under your sssscreen porch ever since you added it. And I can't say I appreciate what I've heard."

"What!"

"All the Ipsssswich chit-chat up there. It's all 'snake in

the grass' this, and 'snake in the grass' that. Every time sssomeone sssuspects a conflict of interest in town government."

"I never said such a thing! I respect our Town leaders!"

"I know that, ssstupid. It's when you read aloud from Facebook."

He had me there.

"You know, I'm the official ssstate reptile of Masssssachusetts," the garter snake continued, "but I don't get any *ressspect*. I work all day, eating your rodents, but do I get any thanks? No. I show my face, and you people ssstop and stare at me, like I'm some kind of freak."

"Sorry," I muttered.

"Eh, I shouldn't complain. The food's good — at least since that wretched outdoor cat of yours died. After you got those two precious new little kittens, and you won't let them ssset food outside, the mice that used to sssecretly run your 200-year-old kitchen every night have been forced outside. I'm eating well."

I shuddered. "Are you sure you're not Satan?"

"Why do you asssk?"

"Well, if you're Satan, I have some questions about lust."

The snake paused.

"If you're asking about your own lust, I'd say go for it," he finally said. "If you're asking about somebody else's lust, it's a terrible thing."

"Why?" I asked.

"Making people judgmental is my ssssspeciality," he hissed. And he slithered off into the lilies of the valley.

A thought for Labor Day week:

This summer — this steamy, sultry, sweaty season of sweltering, of heat, of humidity, of slime on skin, of temperatures I fled after 22 continuous years in the Arizona desert, of idling grumpily in your Volvo on the beach road, of sweltering on the Crane sand and shivering in the Crane surf, of more square miles of exposed flesh than exposed sand, of skin cancer start-ups, this season of abandoning the previous season's swimsuit in favor of something a size larger (or more), and wishing the other person had decided against that swimsuit they're wearing, or trying to wear, this season of bare feet and cuts and splinters and blisters, or ugly flip-flops, this season of children climbing the apple tree risking life and limb, both theirs and the tree's, this season of sunlight invading sleep way too early, of sunny weekdays and rainy weekends, of muck between your toes in Hood Pond, of forgetting to turn off the garden hose and flooding the side yard, this season of big fat juicy garden tomatoes savaged by midnight marauder-deer, of elbows in your ribs at the Marini Farm corn bin, and juicy peaches that my lack of a sweet tooth can't love, this tragic season when oysters are not recommended, this season of Harleys roaring through town and rattling the glass, of bicyclists jarring me awake by yelling at one another as they tear past my bedroom window, of rained-out concerts and even one *heated*-out concert, this season of covering at the office for whoever's on vacation this week, this season of frustratingly foreshortened library hours, of fleas and flies and panting poodles, of greenhead-swatting and Skin So

Soft-slathering, of mosquito-smacking and middle-of-the-night scratching, of bee stings, of ant bites, of lawn-mowing and grass-raking, of tree-pruning and weed-pulling, of poison ivy-ointment-smearing, of pollen-sneezing, of squished worms and frogs and snakes on the road, this season when you open all the windows because the fresh air is so nice, only to get all your stuff soaked when the unexpected rainstorm blows through, when you long for football, and your favorite players get injured in the preseason, when the neighbor's barbecue always smells better than your own, this season of Freon leaks and engine boil-overs and watering bans, this season that lifetime New Englanders adore and live for because they didn't have *22 continuous years of it* in Phoenix —

Yeah, I loved it too.

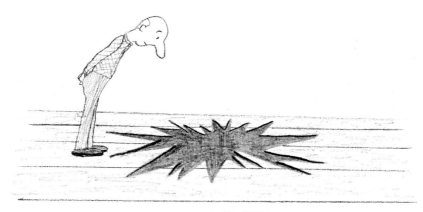

THE LEGEND OF LOBO AND LOUISE

For more than 20 years, living in
Arizona, I slept on a beloved waterbed. It sloshed happily when I climbed into it, and night after night, I drifted

happily to sleep on its gentle waves.

Here in Ipswich, my waterbed is nothing but a bittersweet memory. My vertebrae begin their day complaining. Why? Because of LOBO and LOUISE. They run my life.

You think your life is governed by the Supreme Court, or Mr. Obama? You think your five fine Ipswich selectmen are running your life? You think Robin Crosbie is boss? No. Life is governed by LOBO and LOUISE. Allow me to introduce you.

LOBO is the Law Of Blind Observation. We look at the future, and we think we see it clearly. We think if we look ahead carefully enough, we can somehow control the future, and all will be well.

But all the while, we're actually blind to most of the details. Try as we might, we can't see the future. We don't know what butterfly flapped its wings in China last week, moving a few molecules which then moved another few molecules, until finally, here in Ipswich, it rains on a weekend. We're dutifully observing, but we're governed by LOBO: the Law Of Blind Observation.

Of course, the future isn't all bleak. There are also wonderful surprises. Another butterfly flaps its wings in China, and EBSCO moves to Ipswich. Life is just as full of pleasant surprises as the other kind. We just can't count on them, because we can't see them coming! Because our lives are governed by LOBO: the Law Of Blind Observation.

We're also governed by LOUISE: The Law Of Un-Intended Side-Effects. Even when we get what we expect, it comes with unexpected consequences. Your kid loves you for that video game you bought at Christmas; by Easter you hate your kid for the video game addiction. I claw my way into a great new job, only to find that the travel schedule or the office politics or the "unofficial" expectations make the new job worse than the old one.

Romance is governed by LOUISE, too. You fall in love, you imagine the future with this person, you get married, and then there's the snoring, and the hairs in the bathroom sink, and the cigars. And that's just the wife!

Of course, LOUISE operates the opposite way as well. Expect something bad, discover something good. That new neighbor you didn't like the looks of? Now he's your best buddy. LOUISE has been at work: the Law Of Un-Intended Side-Effects!

LOBO and LOUISE are in charge of my life. They were in charge when I first laid eyes on a 200-year-old house on Linebrook Road. I imagined myself and my family, transplanted from the dreadful desert of Arizona into this cozy, comfortable new milieu. Everything would be as it was, except that now I would drive on winding roads instead of straight, and blow snow instead of grit off my driveway. The differences, I figured, would all be lovely differences.

Then, after taking ownership but before moving in, we walked through the house with an expert restorer of antique properties. Looking at the wide pine floorboards of the second-floor master bedroom, he heard the word "waterbed" and blanched.

"You know what a waterbed weighs?" he asked. "A ton. Literally. Two thousand pounds."

I shifted uneasily on my feet. A floorboard from the John Quincy Adams administration creaked wearily under me.

"You wouldn't put a waterbed up here?" I asked.

"Well, it'll *start* up here," he replied evenly. "But it won't be up here for long. When it crashes through, it'll hit the first floor with quite a bit of speed. Those floorboards are even flimsier than these. You'll be in the cellar before you know it. I'd say 10 seconds, maybe 15."

The cellar. Dirt floor. Spider webs. Not the place for a bedroom.

I love Ipswich, and I love my creaky old house.

I do not love my new, ordinary bed. And I am not really crazy about LOBO and LOUISE.

But I'm stuck with the bed. And we're all stuck with LOBO and LOUISE.

THE WINDS OF WAR, IPSWICH-STYLE

I'm not saying New England is too

windy. Far be it from me to complain about the weather in Ipswich. I chose to live here, of everyplace on the planet. I should not have a problem with wind. I grew up in the Windy City. (Of course, this nickname refers not to Chicago's weather but to its politicians.) Then I spent more than two decades in Phoenix, where massive, ferocious sandstorms blast pebbles into your Pontiac's paint.

So I know wind.

But there does seem to be a certain occasional windiness here in Ipswich, from time to time. Sometimes it's a huge, steady, continuous roar, as if someone in Boxford set up a colossal blow dryer and aimed it toward the east. Other times, it's a quirky, on-again off-again, push-and-pull, gusty-twisty swirl. It blows in your face, then it circles around and blows your glasses off, then circles again and blows in your ear. Tease!

And then of course there are the classic nor'easters, howling in from the Atlantic, turning every North Shore town into Gloucester. "Ahoy, mate!" I scream through the gale to my neighbor across the street. I'm wearing a slicker and leaning forward at a 45-degree angle to get to my mailbox; he's in waders, staggering to keep his footing, to avoid being picked up and blown into my arms like a rag doll.

You can also get what feels like all three winds at once. I had my beloved antique umbrella up over my head in a driving rainstorm, not long ago, tilting into the gale at exactly the right slant to keep the wind and water pounding straight down on the curve of the fabric, when suddenly an invisible arm reached around, slapped my umbrella up from underneath, and instantly turned its beautiful black half-sphere into a ragged, floppy witch's corpse, a dagger pointed at its once-proud owner. Me.

R.I.P.

The unpredictability of Ipswich wind — Ipswind, for short — makes it impossible, in many cases, to completely relax. I put a pub table and four chairs in my backyard, with a crank-operated umbrella stuck through a hole in the table and mounted in a solid metal base on the ground. It was a very fine umbrella (notice I'm using the past tense), a large hexagon of sturdy, reliable fabric in lovely muted earth tones. The shade it provided was broad and dark. A place to relax.

I loved that umbrella. I cranked it up, to reveal its full splendor, when the forecast indicated light winds. I dutifully cranked it back down, into its safe cocoon, if the weatherman predicted anything more than 10 or 12 mph.

But beware: Behind any gentle, seemingly embraceable New England day, there's a stern taskmaster waiting. The Ipswind cometh.

Without warning, my cherished umbrella was cruelly yanked from its moorings. It shot up rocket-like through the hole in the table, arcing over the backyard and plunging like a 1950s-movie flying saucer into my previously pristine peonies.

There is no CPR for a fallen umbrella-comrade.

Spokes bent and broken, fabric savagely shredded. ("Bring out your dead!" Well, this will be "one large object" next to my garbage can next Thursday.)

R.I.P.

(OK, back to business.)

I thought, OK, I'll get some cheap replacement umbrella for my pub table, just for the balance of the season. I went to Wolf Hill — I confess. My townie neighbor recommended against it, because Wolf Hill is *actually* a Gloucester business, carpetbagging at the corner of Route 1 and Linebrook Road in Ipswich. But I live so much closer to Wolf Hill than any of the comparable Ipswich "home and garden centers," I trudged over there.

There was hardly anything left. The backyard pub table season was just about umbrellaed out. But they did have one cheap, wimpy variety of umbrella remaining: far too small for my taste, something like plastic, in a garish neon color completely unfit for staid New England. Plus, forget about shade. This was some sort of thin-weave wanna-be plastic stuff. You sit under this umbrella and look up toward the sun, and your retinas fry like eggs over easy. Just the kind of thing you'd find at a Gloucester business.

Still, the price was right. And summer is short, right? I knew that such a lame umbrella would be up and outa here with the next good stiff New England wind. Probably only days hence. *Whoosh!* And good riddance.

So I bought it. I slid it through the hole in the middle of my pub table. I settled it securely into the solid metal base previously inhabited by the dear departed. I cranked the (obviously inferior) crank to open the (lame neon plastic wanna-be) umbrella to its full deficiency.

And there it stands.

Since that day, we've had hurricanes, we've had nor'easters, we've had special elections — nothing fazes this miserable parasol. It won't bend, it won't tear, it refuses to fly away. I'm too cheap to junk it, too disgusted to get used to it, and too stubborn to change my mind. It stands, steadfast, as a permanent monument to the Ipswind, which blows hither and yon, destroying what it must. And leaving what it will.

THE CIRCLE OF (IPSWICH) LIFE

The circle of life is a beautiful thing,

except when it's not. Bloody-faced lions gobbling zebra guts, for example, are part of the circle of life, but I have to look away. (My middle-schooler loves this stuff.)

Ipswich has its own circle of life, which fortunately does not involve the gobbling of anybody's guts. It's a three-stage circle, and here's how it goes:

Stage 1. We're driving along, minding our own business, when suddenly a colossal *thunk* wrenches the steering wheel from our grasp, and we realize there's a major new pothole where there wasn't one before, and we'll have to remember to steer around it next time. But we don't remember, and we go *thunk* again, and we cuss. Then another pothole appears, not too far away, and then another. We learn to drive slowly on this stretch of road. We pick our way through the war zone, our Chrysler creeping among the land mines. Eventually, however, the plethora of potholes is so annoying that we actually pick up the phone and dial Town Hall and complain.

In this activity, we citizens are functioning as the bottom of the food chain, like mice, or grasshoppers, creatures that don't strike fear in the heart of other creatures, but rather, for the most part, get eaten by them. We are almost entirely powerless. Most of us don't have the wherewithal to fill our own potholes. We can't protest by withholding our tax dollars, because it will wind up costing us even more in attorneys' fees. All we can do is mutter, and soldier on, and — at the very most — squawk.

But this is not the end of the cycle. It's only just begun. The Ipswich circle of life continues. Next, on the second floor of Town Hall, we find our intrepid Town Manager frowning into her computer screen. She has a million problems to worry about — it's like flies harassing a wildebeest. The moment she shoos one with her tail, another lands on her nose. You just get FinCom settled down, and the Rec Committee is on you. Now, on top of all this, there's the nagging little buzzing sound of citizens calling to complain about a certain passel of potholes. Finally, the buzzing reaches critical mass. The Town Manager grabs her phone. She barks into the handset: "Get me the pothole guys." Soon, the pothole SWAT team descends on the much-maligned stretch of street. The hot black glop oozes, the smoothing specialists do their smoothing, and the plague is finally over. You can glide on this street now. You could land a small plane. You can rollerblade in your sleep. You can speed.

Stage 2. We're walking along, minding our own business, on our nice new level road, when a Harley roars past, doing about 55. A soccer mom in an SUV whooshes past you like a shark. Delivery truck roars by. Kid at the wheel, escaping chores, heading for his girlfriend's house, passes in a blur. Old guy in an antique convertible: *Raaaaaarrr!*

This is the stage where drivers, freed from the menacing moonscape, put the pedal to the metal. It's such a joy to sail over level blacktop without fear of rack-and-pinion ruination that you can't stop yourself. You speed.

But this is not the end of Stage 2. Oh my, no. The Ipswich circle of life continues. On Elm Street, inside a very old building, on a massive multi-paneled console, tiny lights are lighting up, and a diligent young man in an Ipswich Police Department uniform is trying very hard to answer all the phone calls.

"Yes, ma'am, thank you, got it."

"Yes, sir, thank you. I'll let him know."

The problem with the high-tech console at the Ipswich Police Department is that it doesn't have a "Send to voicemail" button.

The young man finally rips the headset off, throws it aside, and lunges into Chief Nikas's office.

"Everyone's complaining about the speeders!"

Chief Nikas is a calm soul. Like the wise gorilla father overseeing his troop of little gorillas in the jungle, he knows what to get exercised about, and what not to.

"Well done, grasshopper," he says to the boy. "Keep treating them nicely."

He waves the boy out. The people complaining about speeders are probably the same ones who vote against new police cruisers and more police officers. How do you patrol 42 square miles with so few cops in such old cars? Resources must be expended wisely. Stop a speeder on School Street on Saturday, miss a murder on Mitchell on Monday.

Still, the cries of the citizens, squalling about speeders, are not without effect. Someone else hears them. Someone higher up than the wildebeest, higher up than the gorilla.

Stage 3. Mother Nature, sitting in an ancient La-Z-Boy on her celestial screen porch, finishes the last gulp of gin, plunks the glass down on a rickety side table, picks up a pack of Winstons and knocks one out. Lighting it, she rasps out of the side of her mouth: "Bring me another, will ya, honey?" Her husband grunts from the kitchen. Most people don't realize that Mother Nature is married to St. Peter.

She has the craggy look of a woman who's been out

in the sun a lot. Her duties don't allow her a lot of indoors-time.

Soon St. Peter ambles out of the house in his undershirt. He hands her another gin on the rocks, drops himself into the rocking chair next to her, and takes a glug of his Corona. It would be a good life up here, except for the noise. There's an almost constant array of sounds coming up from below — sort of a buzzing, whining, clicking, ticking, clucking — the sound of human grievance.

"They're making me crazy," St. Peter mumbles.

"It's the speeders," Mother Nature replies, her voice scratching like steel wool.

"Well, do something about it!" her husband snarls.

Mother Nature sighs heavily, smoke streaming out of her nostrils. She groans as she leans forward to pull herself out of the lounger, and a string of gray hair slips down in her face. She stubs out her butt, shuffles to the door of the screen porch, pushes it open, and steps down to her front yard — which is basically a cloud. She crosses her arms, then arcs them out wide. The cloud-yard turns gray, then smoky black. She turns back toward the house, climbs the steps onto the screen porch, drops into the La-Z-Boy.

"Whadja do to 'em?" St. Peter asks.

"Winterized the bastards," she snorts. "Snow, ice, sleet, hail, fog. Standard New England winter. Can't speed in that stuff."

"Hm," St. Peter murmurs.

"What?" she grumps. "You don't even thank me?" She picks up her glass. "Aw, hell. Get me another one, will ya, honey?"

Stage 3. Down on the street, winter falls. Snow howls

out of the sky. Hail hails and sleet sleets. Ice stretches over the asphalt like deadly cellophane. Fog cloaks the danger in a secret shroud.

None of which slows the New England drivers a bit. They race through town, engines roaring, their death-machines flying over the slippery glare, doing 40 where the signs say 25, as if they're brilliant mathematicians and simply assume the signs are written in base 16. The complaining continues, and St. Peter keeps grumbling.

But this is Stage 3 of the Ipswich circle of life, and well under the snow, well beneath the ice, well below the surface of the asphalt, things are not well. The black semisolid bituminous road-surfacing blacktop, which began life happily in a sizzling construction company vat at solar-storm temperatures, is now shivering pathetically under its frigid bedspread. The moisture trickles into every wrinkle, the freezing painfully presses every vein, the asphalt cracks and crumbles, its strength slipping, its spirit broken.

And in the spring, as the speeders dash over the fragments, the corpse begins hollowing out. A flaw opens into a gap. A crack becomes a cavity. Until soon we have something Mother Nature never intended — she was only trying to slow down the speeders. Now, once again, we have potholes.

Another unexpected *thunk* of that right front tire. Another unanticipated cussword. And the Ipswich circle of life is complete.

Or rather, it begins anew.

LEARNING TO DRAW *Town Manager Robin...*

Ode to the Town Manager

I am an unabash-ed fan
Of Robin Crosbie, our Town Man-

           ager.

Our Town is better than it was
Before, in no small part because

           of her.

She's strictly business. This you knew.
And yet, she also has a hu-

           man side.

She loves to dance, to party, or
To take the new police boat for

           a ride.

Her work she pours herself into.
Our town she is committed to

           enrich.

But yes, it's hard keep a grip,
In light of how some folks in Ip-

           swich bitch.

So Robin labors, all alone,
Without considering her own

           renown.

She wants the world to know what's true:
We are the finest Massachu-

           setts town.

I'm glad to see her persevere,
Excelling in her manageer-

           rial rule.

She does not live for our applause,
And that's why I say Robin Cros-

           bie's cool.

Thou Shalt Love

Thy
Town Manager

CREDIT DUE

Thanks to Dan MacAlpine, editor of the *Ipswich Chronicle*, who graciously invited me to this "columnist" role, and thereafter patiently tolerated me.

And to my wife Kristina Brendel, who serves as "first reader" for every column I produce, and usually makes her comments without devastating me. My readers owe her.

And special thanks to my faithful volunteer copy editor, Sarah Christine Jones, of Wadsworth, Ohio, who doesn't necessarily get New England small-town humor, but knows a dangling participle when she sees one.

DougBrendel.com | NEW THING.net | *Time & Tide fine Art*

LET US CONNECT

Doug's contact info is at DougBrendel.com.
More about his columns: Outsidah.com.
Look for Doug on Facebook, Twitter, Pinterest, and
    everywhere fine writers are sold.
Doug's wife Kristina owns TimeAndTideFineArt.com.
Their ministry in the former USSR is NewThing.net.
Please contact us. It's lonely in outer Linebrook.

The material in this book is just Doug Brendel's. He writes as a volunteer for the *Ipswich Chronicle*, so anything in this book that also appeared in the *Chronicle* is Doug's responsibility. Don't blame the newspaper.

This book also has no official connection whatsoever to GateHouse Media, the *Ipswich Chronicle*'s parent company. Doug, however, unofficially reveres GateHouse, and does everything he can to keep them happy. Within reason.

Also, please note: *No clams were fried in the printing of this book.*

www.DougBrendel.com